More Creative Encounters

ACTIVITIES TO EXPAND CHILDREN'S RESPONSES TO LITERATURE

Anne T. Polkingharn and Catherine Toohey
Illustrated by Lynn Welker

LIBRARIES UNLIMITED, INC.
Englewood, Colorado
1988

LIBRARIES UNLIMITED, INC.
P.O. Box 3988
Englewood, Colorado 80155-3988

Library of Congress Cataloging-in-Publication Data

Polkingharn, Anne T., 1937-
    More creative encounters : activities to expand children's
responses to literature / Anne T. Polkingharn and Catherine Toohey ;
illustrated by Lynn Welker.
        x, 116 p. 22x28 cm.
        Bibliography: p. 111
        Includes index.
        ISBN 0-87287-663-2
        1. Children--Books and reading.   2. Children's literature--Study
and teaching (Elementary)   3. Libraries, Children's--Activity
programs.   4. Elementary school libraries--Activity programs.
5. Activity programs in education.   I. Toohey, Catherine, 1949-   .
II. Title.
Z1037.A1P62 1988
372.6--dc19   88-8892
                                                                              CIP

Libraries Unlimited books are bound with Type II nonwoven material that meets and exceeds National Association of State Textbook Administrators' Type II nonwoven material specifications Class A through E.

To Jane and Linda—for being friends and sisters.

Table of Contents

Preface

More Creative Encounters is a children's literature idea book for elementary grades providing activities for specific book titles which children enjoy. Recent research continues to point out what teachers and librarians have always known: Literature in the classroom is essential if children are to benefit from the written word. Schools are implementing response-based literature programs. Teachers are seeking literature enrichment activities. Programs in which listening, speaking, reading, writing, and the study of literature are mutually taught are being incorporated into school curriculums. *Becoming a Nation of Readers* states "There is no substitute for a teacher who reads children good stories. It whets the appetite of children for reading, and provides a model of skillful oral reading. It is a practice that should continue through the grades."[1]

In *Creative Encounters* published by Libraries Unlimited in 1983 and *More Creative Encounters*, we have developed and presented response-based literature activities for books children enjoy. The fifty-one books we have selected are recent publications available in school and public libraries as well as in bookstores. These are books and activities that we use. The activities require ordinary classroom materials that are utilized to help children reason, draw, write, research, repeat language patterns, and make personal interpretations of the literature.

This book is organized so that the entry for each book title includes a summary of the particular book, explains a purpose for the related activity, provides a list of the materials needed for the activity, and step-by-step instructions for completing the activity. The "Notes" section includes additional suggestions for the teacher and related book titles. Further bibliographic information about each title is found at the end of the book. Teachers and librarians find these activities easy to use and especially effective in that children remember these books and want to read them again.

Our purpose is to provide imaginative activities that familiarize teachers and librarians with the wealth of materials awaiting children on library shelves. In the past, beginning readers have been given few opportunities to respond effectively to the literature they have read or heard. The books we have chosen to include in *More Creative Encounters* are excellent materials for integrating language arts and literature into the classroom. In choosing each book, we have considered the child's interest, suitability and grade level of each title, originality, depth of content, appropriateness of illustration and use of language. We have read many books, book reviews, and lists of recommended books. Our experiences as librarian and classroom teacher have reinforced our knowledge of books and our belief that children want to respond to what they read and incorporate reading into their personal experience. Best of all books are a source of intense enjoyment and can be shared with other children and adults. Our focus in these activities is on the relationship of the student to the content of the book. The teacher's role is to explain the activity, provide the materials necessary, enrich the student's response, and clarify student questions. By sharing books and response-based literature activities, teachers provide opportunities for developing thinking skills. Each child's response will be unique and can be shared with other children. Many of these activities provide bulletin board materials created by students that can be displayed to reinforce books and reading.

Students of all ability levels benefit from these extension activities. These books become associated with pleasureable reading activities, not drill and practice, thus making reading a positive experience for the child. In addition these book-related activities extend the reading of the book and demonstrate to students, parents, and administrators how much the teacher values the recreational reading program. Students want help in selecting "good" books and these activities are based on books children enjoy.

Our concern in school is that children develop thinking, listening, and communicating skills. These skills are not learned in isolation but should be correlated with activities demanding these skills so learning is relevant and can be reinforced through application. These activities provide these skills and application while students enjoy the reading of a book.

From *A, My Name Is Alice* to *Humphrey the Lost Whale: A True Story*, students learn to appreciate a variety of literature. These books and literature-based activities in *More Creative Encounters* motivate students to create, explore, think, and remember. Reading and writing skills improve as children follow directions, create, and share their results with each other. As children discover the joy of reading, they also experience the pleasure of thinking, laughing, and learning from the books they choose.

NOTES

[1]John C. Manning, *Becoming a Nation of Readers: Implications for School Reading Programs* (Scott, Foresman, 1900).

Marianna May and Nursey

TOMIE DE PAOLA

(Holiday House, 1983)

Marianna May is a poor little rich girl who is always dressed in white. Marianna May is scolded by Nursey when she gets her white dresses soiled with ice cream, mud pies, and paint. The solution to the problem of soiled dresses is much to Marianna May's delight

PURPOSE:

This activity allows children to recreate a play situation in which Marianna May soils her dress. The children use a pattern to recreate Tomie de Paola's art style and Marianna's solution to her problem.

MATERIALS:

(1) copy of Marianna May's dress pattern
Crayons or marking pens
Scissors
Glue
Butcher paper

LET'S BEGIN:

1. Read *Marianna May and Nursey*.
2. Think of an additional situation Marianna May could have encountered in her white dress.
3. Color the dress pattern to reflect the results of Marianna May's activity. Leave the waistband white.
4. On the waistband write the activity Marianna May was engaged in.
5. On the butcher paper draw a simple clothesline with two poles and a line long enough to hold everyone's dress pattern.
6. Cut the dresses out and glue them below the clothesline.

NOTES:

For a writing activity staple the pattern at the shoulders onto a piece of writing paper. Cut the pattern and writing paper for an instant shape book. Older students may write about Marianna May's further adventures or what they felt about her predicament.

Tomie de Paola has written and illustrated over 100 books for children. All will have their favorite titles—here are a few:

Strega Nona: An Old Tale
The Legend of the Bluebonnet
Charlie Needs a Cloak
Bill and Pete
Big Anthony and the Magic Ring

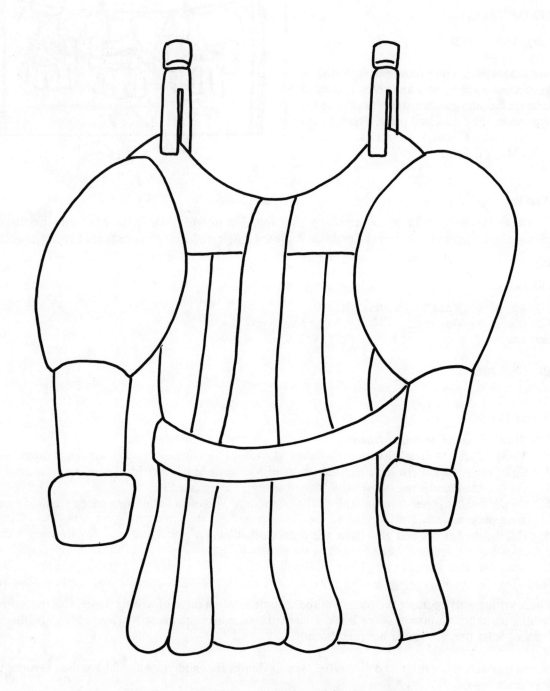

Marianna May and Nursey
by Tomie de Paola

The Very Busy Spider

ERIC CARLE

(Philomel, 1984)

The very busy spider is diligent about spinning her web in spite of attempts by other farm animals to divert her. She produces a beautiful and useful web that can be felt as well as seen.

PURPOSE:

Children appreciate the spider's skill and feel the raised web on each page as the spider progresses in her web spinning. Each child will create a web that is raised and touchable on a paper plate. The spider will be added.

MATERIALS:

(1) paper plate—not a waxed or styrofoam plate
White glue
Powdered black tempera paint
Marking pens
Plastic squeeze bottle

LET'S BEGIN:

1. In a plastic squeeze bottle, mix two teaspoons powdered black tempera paint with four tablespoons white glue. The mixture should be the consistency of thick white glue and easy to draw with. This amount of glue/paint mixture will be used to paint one spider web.
2. Read *The Very Busy Spider*.
3. Using the plastic squeeze bottle, draw a black spider's web on a paper plate. Allow time for the glue/paint to dry.
4. Add a spider on the web with marking pens.
5. Write the title of the book around the edge of the plate.
6. Feel the raised web with your fingers.

NOTES:

You can relate this lesson to Braille writing and the sense of touching the page and feeling the raised web which is similar to feeling the raised dots of Braille writing.

With younger children the teacher draws the spider's web with the paint/glue mixture on a piece of large mural paper. Each child adds a spider with marking pens. Print the title of the book on the mural.

Read other stories by Eric Carle.

Related books:
  Be Nice to Spiders, by Margaret Lee Graham
  The Spider Makes a Web, by Joan Lexau
  Spider's Web, by Christine Back
  Wolfie, by Janet Chenery
  The Spider's Dance, by Joanne Ryder
  Fresh Cider and Pie, by Franz Brandenberg
  Spiders, by Illa Podendorf

Arthur's Eyes

MARC BROWN

(Little, Brown, 1979)

Arthur has difficulty seeing and goes to see Dr. Iris, the optometrist. Arthur is told he needs glasses. His friends tease Arthur about his glasses, but after some resistance, talking to his teacher, and seeing Francine in her pink movie-star glasses, Arthur begins wearing his glasses with pride.

PURPOSE:

Children appreciate the problems that Arthur encounters wearing glasses. Each child makes and wears a pair of glasses that he or she designs. This story is helpful to children in the class who wear glasses reluctantly.

MATERIALS:

(1) 6x9-inch piece of tagboard
Marking pens
Hole punch
Cellophane tape
(1) 3x6-inch piece of transparent colored plastic
Scissors

LET'S BEGIN:

1. Read *Arthur's Eyes*.
2. Give a piece of tagboard to each child with circles for the eyes drawn on it to make glasses. The diameter of the circles should be two inches. To assist the children in cutting out the circles, punch a single hole inside the circle so that there is a starting place for the scissor points to cut out the entire circle. Cut out a circle for each eye.
3. Design glasses and decorate them with marking pens.
4. Place a strip of colored plastic behind the holes in the glasses and tape the plastic strip to the back of the glasses.
5. Try on the glasses, looking through the colored plastic.

NOTES:

We used strips of colored plastic report or notebook folders. They are available in school or office supply stores in red, blue, green, and yellow.

Children love to work with glitter. If you would like to add a glamorous look to movie-star glasses such as those worn by Francine in the story, you may order glitter pens from:

Childcraft
20 Kilmer Road
Edison, NJ 08818
1-800-631-5657

Related books:

Katie's Magic Glasses, by Jane Goodsell
Spectacles, by Ellen Raskin
Mr. Turtle's Magic Glasses, by Catherine Wooley
Two Strikes, Four Eyes, by Ned Delaney
Cromell's Glasses, by Holly Keller
Libby's New Glasses, by Tricia Tusa

Join the Arthur Fan Club. Write to:

ARTHUR
c/o Little, Brown and Company
34 Beacon Street
Boston, MA 02108-1493.

I Unpacked My Grandmother's Trunk

SUSAN RAMSAY HOGUET

(Dutton, 1983)

Based on the alphabet memory game concerning packing for a trip, this book engages and delights the reader.

PURPOSE:

This activity allows children to individualize grandmother's trunk and involves the class in a game of memory.

MATERIALS:

(1) 12x18-inch piece of white construction paper
Alphabet stencils
Crayons or marking pens

LET'S BEGIN:

1. Read *I Unpacked My Grandmother's Trunk.*
2. Fold the construction paper so that 3 inches are left uncovered.

3. Write "I unpacked my grandmother's trunk, and out of it I took" across the top piece.
4. Choose an alphabet stencil and trace it below the sentence.
5. Draw a trunk on the side of the page so that the locks and opening fall on the opening of the paper.

6. Open up the page and draw something imaginative that begins with the letter on the cover.

7. Arrange the class set of letters in alphabetical order to form a book. Read or play a memory game with this class book.

NOTES:

Other ABC books to enjoy are:
I Can Be the Alphabet, by Marinella Bonini
The Ultimate Alphabet, by Mike Wilks
Teachers: A to Z, by Jean Johnson
Alphabatics, by Suse MacDonald

Owl Lake

TEJIMA

(Philomel, 1982)

A lake shimmers as the sun sets. A family of owls begins to stir. Dramatic woodcuts show the owls in bold, black, detailed pictures. The Father Owl flies out across the lake to catch a fish to feed his family.

PURPOSE:

Children appreciate the nighttime world of the owl and the woodcut illustrations used in this book. Each child scratches a picture on black scratchboard depicting a scene from nature.

MATERIALS:

8-inch square piece of tagboard
Crayons in hot colors (yellow, orange, and red)
Black tempera paint and brush
Liquid soap
Wood stick or bamboo skewer

To make scratchboard:
1. Cover the tagboard with a thick layer of crayon. You can use a variety of hot colors in any design you wish—stripes, squares, circles, etc.
2. Wipe off the crumbs of crayon.
3. Mix one cup of black liquid tempera paint with two tablespoons of liquid soap. The liquid soap will help the paint to adhere to the crayon wax.
4. Paint over the crayon area as smoothly as possible with the black tempera paint. Paint in one direction to cover the crayon area.
5. Let the scratchboard dry. Now it is ready to be scratched with a wood stick or bamboo skewer.

Commercially prepared Scratch-Art paper and scratch-etchboard may be ordered from:
  Scratch-Art Company, Inc.
  460 Dedham Street
  Newton Center, MA 02159

Wood sticks to be used as scratching tools may also be ordered from this company. As a substitute for the wood stick, use T-pins, cuticle sticks, or bamboo skewers.

LET'S BEGIN:

1. Read *Owl Lake*.
2. Talk about the illustrations in the book, pointing out the fine detail in the owl's feathers, the sky, the trees, etc. Call attention to the small marks which the artist has used to enhance the illustrations.
3. Using the scratchboard you have made or purchased scratchboard and a wood stick, scratch a nature scene. Include an animal in your picture.

NOTES:

Children may practice scratching short lines on newsprint before trying this technique on the scratchboard.

When drawing an animal on scratchboard, it is helpful to outline the animal with dots before filling in the details of the animal.

Read *Fox's Dream*, by Tejima. The story tells of a cold and hungry fox who is reminded of a springtime past when he was not alone. The illustrations are similar to those in *Owl Lake*.

The Jolly Postman or Other People's Letters

JANET AHLBERG AND ALLAN AHLBERG

(Little, Brown, 1986)

A very Jolly Postman delivers letters to some of our favorite fairy- and folk-tale characters. The actual letters can be taken from the envelopes in the book. This imaginative book delights children and adults alike.

PURPOSE:

This activity involves students in a letter-writing assignment following the humorous theme of this book.

MATERIALS:

(1) piece of writing paper/stationery
(1) envelope
(1) stamp or 1-inch square of paper

LET'S BEGIN:

1. Read *The Jolly Postman or Other People's Letters.*
2. Choose a familiar character from a well-known story to write a letter to.
3. As part of the prewriting step list the characteristics and problems the chosen character has.
4. Draft a letter, keeping in mind the characteristics of the characters and imagining what they would write about in their correspondence.
5. Revise your letter carefully and rewrite it on a decorated piece of stationery that would look appropriate for the character you choose.
6. Address the envelope, keeping in mind the details about your book character.
7. Attach the stamp and place the letter in the envelope.

NOTES:

Suggestions for characters to write to include:
Rapunzel, Peter Rabbit, one of the Three Pigs, Princess from *The Princess and the Pea.*

For book reports or character analysis students may want to write to more contemporary characters from current books: Ramona, Beezus, Cam Jansen, Encyclopedia Brown, Einstein Anderson.

For younger students read a folk or fairy tale and write a group letter to the appropriate character.

Other books that revolve around letter writing are:
  Please Send Panda, by Ruth Orbach
  Dear Hildegarde, by Bernard Waber
  Mailbox, Quailbox, by Margaret R. Legum
  What the Mailman Brought, by Carolyn Craven

Older students will enjoy:
  Dear Mr. Henshaw, by Beverly Cleary

When Panda Came to Our House

HELEN ZANE JENSEN

(Dial, 1985)

A panda from faraway China comes to visit an American girl. They become great friends. The panda teaches the girl many things about China. This book includes a glossary of Chinese characters and definitions. Chinese characters are used to enhance the illustrations and are related to the content of the story.

PURPOSE:

Young children hear the story and are introduced to the meaning of the Chinese characters in the upper left-hand corner of each illustration. One Chinese character represents the English word "fan."

There are two kinds of fans that people in China use. The round fan does not fold and is usually used by women. Men prefer the folding fan that came to China from Japan. Children practice writing the Chinese character for "fan" and make a fan.

MATERIALS:

(1) round fan pattern for each round fan
(1) piece of 9x7-inch tagboard for each round fan
(1) tongue depressor for handle of the round fan
(1) piece of 9x12-inch construction paper for each accordion-folded fan
Marking pens
Glue
Scissors

LET'S BEGIN:

1. Read *When Panda Came to Our House.*
2. Practice writing the Chinese character for "fan," as seen in the book.

3. Choose to make a round tagboard fan and write the Chinese character for "fan" on it, or choose to make an accordion-folded paper fan with the Chinese character for "fan" on it.
4. If you choose the round fan, cut the round fan out of tagboard using the pattern page. Glue the tongue depressor handle to the round fan shape.
5. If you choose the folded fan, accordion fold the paper fan after writing the Chinese character "fan" on it.

NOTES:

Older students will enjoy *The Great Wall of China*, by Leonard Everett Fisher. See Chinese characters on p. 32 (last page).

Related books:
    You Can Write Chinese, by Kurt Wiese
    Chinese in 10 Minutes a Day, by Kristine Kershul
    Alphabet Art: Thirteen ABC's from around the World, by Leonard Everett Fisher
    Chinese Mother Goose Rhymes, by Robert Utley Hyndman

    Chinese word for horse. Media Guild. 12 min. film.

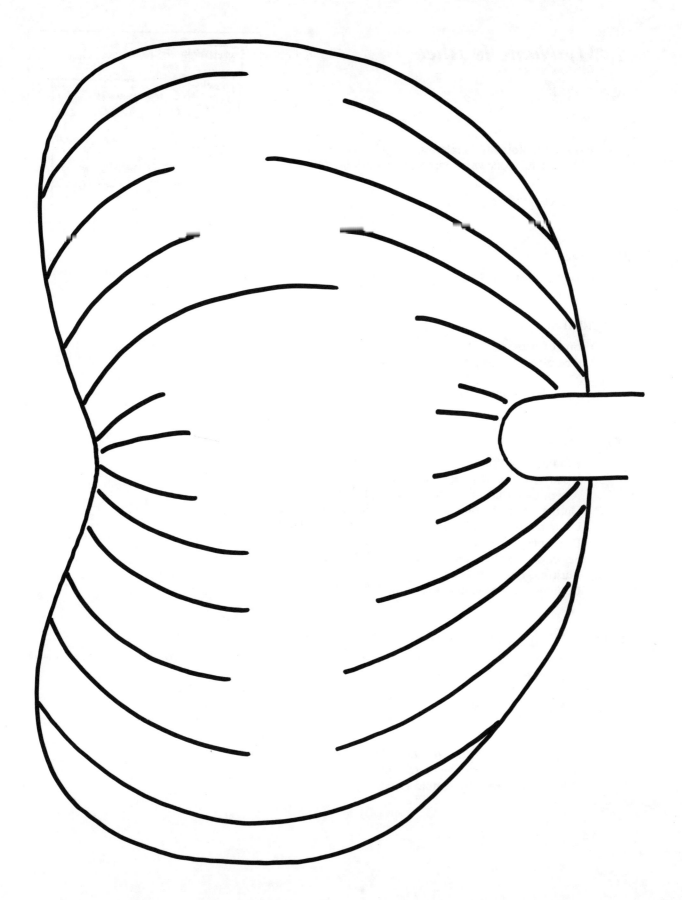

A, My Name Is Alice

JANE BAYER

(Dial, 1987)

This is a silly and informative alphabet book children are certain to enjoy. Each letter follows a simple pattern of alliteration.

PURPOSE:

Students brainstorm, write, and make their own books following the language pattern of the book.

MATERIALS:

(1) copy of pattern
(1) piece of writing paper
Pencil
Reference books and encyclopedias

LET'S BEGIN:

1. Read *A, My Name Is Alice*.
2. Discover the playful repetitious pattern and alliteration.
3. Assign each student a letter of the alphabet.
4. On the top of the outline page write the assigned letter.
5. Using reference books and encyclopedias, fill in the chart.
6. Experiment with the information gathered to fill in the pattern from *A, My Name Is Alice*.
7. Select one combination and write that sentence for the class book.
8. Illustrate your sentence.
9. Combine each page into a class alphabet book.

NOTES:

With younger children this can be done as a group writing experience. This project may be done by several children working on one letter.

Other ABC books to enjoy are:
Alligators All Around, by Maurice Sendak
Have You Ever Seen...? An ABC Book, by Beau Gardner
Ashanti to Zulu: African Traditions, by Margaret Musgrove
Halloween ABC, by Eve Merriman
On Market Street, by Arnold Lobel

My letter is _____ .

Female names:

1.
2.
3.
4.
5.

Male names:

1.
2.
3.
4.
5.

Animals

1.
2.
3.
4.
5.

Unusual items

1.
2.
3.
4.
5.

Cities

1.
2.
3.
4.
5.

_____My name is _____ and my husband's name is _____ . We live in _____ and we sell _____ .

Need a House?
Call Ms. Mouse!

GEORGE MENDOZA

(Grosset & Dunlap, 1981)

Henrietta is a famous designer, architect, dreamer, and builder. This book shows the variety of homes and environments that she has designed, such as Mole's manor, Cat's villa, Owl's tower, and Squirrel's treehouse. On the final page of the book Henrietta admits that she likes the simple life and asks the reader, "How about you?"

PURPOSE:

Each child completes the pattern for a folded house. Children design a house that they would like to live in. It may be a dream house, a real house, or an animal's house showing rooms, staircases, windows, furniture, doors, etc.

MATERIALS:

(1) 12x18-inch piece of white construction paper
Marking pens or crayons
Scissors
Ruler

LET'S BEGIN:

1. Read *Need a House? Call Ms. Mouse!*
2. Fold the white piece of construction paper. Fold the left side to the center and crease. Fold the right side to the center and crease.
3. Cut triangle shapes from each side of the folded paper. Cut from the fold to the top center on each side.

4. Design the rooms in the house, the staircase, windows, doors, interior furniture, artwork, closets, attic, basement, etc.
5. On the back of the interior of the house, design the exterior of the house. Include your name, complete home address, and telephone number.

NOTES:

This project makes an interesting bulletin board for an open house.

Related books:
  The Little House, by Virginia Lee Burton
  A House Is a House for Me, by Mary Ann Hoberman
  The Room, by Mordicai Gerstein
  The Snug Little House, by Eils Morehouse Lewis

Humbug Potion,
an A B Cipher

LORNA BALIAN

(Abingdon, 1984)

An ugly witch dearly wishes to be beautiful. She discovers an old recipe for a Magic Beauty Potion. The recipe is written in code. Page by page the witch concocts the recipe, but leaves out one very important ingredient … a smile.

New Humbug Potion
by Meghann McNaught

Drop	13-21-4
Add	7-15-15
Sift	4-21-19-20
Cut in	19-12-9-13-5
Flavor with	22-1-14-9-12-12-1
Toss in	13-5-7-8-1-14-14

Stir carefully- strain through a torn stocking- and DRINK EVERY DROP.

PURPOSE:

This project allows students to cooperatively decipher what the witch was mixing in her potion. The project also engages students in a creative writing assignment using the witch's code.

MATERIALS:

(40) 6x1-inch strips of paper
Code sheet
(1) copy of the code
(1) copy of the recipe worksheet

LET'S BEGIN:

1. Prepare strips of paper with the code word from each page in the book. The complete list of coded words is on page 24.
2. Pass out the strips of paper along with a copy of the code (page 23). Some children may get more than one strip.
3. Allow children time to decode their strip by writing the letters below the numbers.

20-5-5-20-8
teeth

4. Assemble the children with their decoded strips and begin reading *Humbug Potion*. Read the first code slowly and allow children time to see if they have that particular code. Let each child fill in the story as his or her code is read.
5. Each child has an opportunity to participate in the story as you read. Everyone will enjoy the witch's concoction.
6. As a follow-up students can invent their own ingredients in code for another witch's brew.
7. Write the new ingredients on the recipe pattern.
8. Trade papers and let children decode each other's recipes.

NOTES:

This writing part of the project makes an unusual homework assignment.

This project can be done over a period of several days.

The reading of the story proceeds quickly as students begin to see the pattern of the code and then to anticipate their participation.

Other books by Lorna Balian:
Humbug Witch
Humbug Rabbit
Sometimes It's Turkey, Sometimes It's Feathers
Leprechauns Never Lie
Bah! Humbug
If I Had Long, Long Hair

Related books about codes:
The Case of the Double Cross, by Crosby Bonsall
The Secret Three, by Mildred Myrick
How to Keep a Secret: Writing and Talking in Code, by Elizabeth James and Carol Barkin
The Code & Cipher Book, by Jane Sanoff and Reynold Ruffins

Recipe Pattern <u>Humbug Potion</u>
by Lorna Balian

Drop
Add
Sift
Cut in
Flavor with
Toss in

 Stir carefully- strain through a torn stocking- and DRINK EVERY DROP.

HUMBUG POTION
an A·B· Cipher

by Lorna Balian

		a 1	b 2	c 3	d 4
e 5	f 6	g 7	h 8	i 9	j 10
k 11	l 12	m 13	n 14	o 15	p 16
q 17	r 18	s 19	t 20	u 21	v 22
w 23	x 24	y 25	z 26		

Code Sheet

Codes from *Humbug Potion, an A B Cipher* by Lorna Balian

1-3-15-18-14	7-18-1-16-5-19	15-14-9-15-14	20-5-5-20-8
2-9-20	8-1-9-18	16-1-9-12	21-13-2-18-5-12-12-1
2-18-15-15-13	8-5-14	16-5-1-19	19-13-9-12-5
3-21-16	9-14-19-5-3-20	17-21-9-12-12	22-9-15-12-5-20-19
3-15-4	10-1-18	17-21-1-9-12	23-1-20-5-18
4-18-25	10-5-12-12-25	18-5-4-	23-15-15-12
4-9-18-20	11-5-25	18-9-2-15-14	23-15-12-6
5-7-7-19	12-1-3-5	19-15-1-16	11-9-19-19-5-19
6-9-19-8	13-15-21-19-5	19-8-15-5	25-15-25-15
7-18-5-5-14	14-1-9-12	20-23-15	26-9-14-14-9-1

Lion

WILLIAM PÈNE DU BOIS

(Viking, 1983)

Foreman is an artist who works in heaven in an animal factory. He designs animals to be flown to the planets of the universe. The story relates the artistic and design procedures for designing the animal we call "lion."

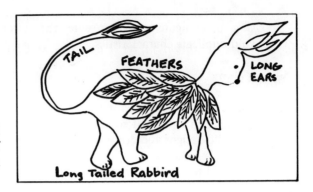

PURPOSE:

Using the computer in a language arts experience allows children an opportunity to design an animal as Foreman did in the story.

MATERIALS:

Marking pens
Pencils
Computer with printer and 8½x11-inch form-feed paper
If you do not have access to a computer you can do this project another way. Write the animal characteristics on index cards and have each child randomly select three index cards to use. Each child designs an animal showing the three characteristics he or she has selected. Children draw and name the animal they have designed.

LET'S BEGIN:

Session One

1. Read *Lion*.
2. Divide the children into groups. Each group should think of physical characteristics of animals and make a list of animal characteristics. Examples: hair, tail, trunk, spout, mouth, pouch, feathers, beak, long ears, fins, etc.
3. The computer program is written in APPLESOFT BASIC. Animal characteristics are included in line 400. You may enter more than ten characteristics by adjusting line 5.

```
5 CLASS = 10
20   HOME
30   INPUT "What is your name? ";N$
35   HOME
40   PR# 1
45   PRINT N$;", design an animal with:"
47   PRINT
50   FOR L = 1 TO 3
60   R = INT ( RND (1) * CLASS + 1)
70   FOR W = 1 TO R
80   READ W$
90   NEXT W
100    PRINT W$
110    RESTORE
120    NEXT L
140    FOR L = 1 TO 62
150    PRINT ""
160    NEXT L
170    PR# 0
180    GOTO 20
400    DATA  a trunk,a pouch,long ears,a long neck,a beak,feathers,fins,a
       tail, a spout,hair
```

25

Using the computer program, enter the animal characteristics provided by the children in line 400. Avoid duplicate characteristics.

Session Two

4. Each child types his or her name on the computer. The program assigns three animal characteristics to each child on a piece of computer paper. Example: long ears, feathers, tail.
5. Each child designs and draws an imaginary animal on the piece of computer paper showing these three characteristics.
6. Each child names the animal he or she designed.

NOTES:

This lesson is best done in two sessions with some computer time in between.

The children may design as many of these animals as they wish. They will receive three different animal characteristics each time they type their name in the computer.

This book may be used with a nonfiction animal unit in which children study animal characteristics and classification.

Related books:
  Benny's Animals and How He Put Them in Order, by Millicent E. Selsam
  You Look Ridiculous Said the Rhinoceros to the Hippopotamus, by Bernard Waber
  McBroom's Zoo, by Sid Fleischman
  One More and One Less, by Betsy Giulio Maestro
  As I Was Crossing Boston Common, by Norma Farber

My thanks to the computer literacy teachers at our school — and yours, too!

If You Give a Mouse a Cookie

LAURA JOFFE NUMEROFF

(Harper & Row, 1985)

A humorous story that emphasizes cause and effect beginning with what will happen if you offer a cookie to a mouse.

PURPOSE:

This activity provides students with a way to recognize cause and effect through creative dramatics.

MATERIALS:

(20) 12x6-inch strips of tagboard
(20) 24-inch strips of ribbon or yarn
Marking pen
Hole punch
Masking tape

LET'S BEGIN:

1. Read *If You Give a Mouse a Cookie.*
2. On each strip of tagboard write one of the nineteen items listed in the story: child, mouse, cookie, milk, straw, napkin, mirror, scissors, broom, box, blanket, pillow, story, paper, crayons, picture, pen, Scotch tape, and refrigerator.
3. Punch two holes in the top of each name strip.
4. Thread and tie the yarn or ribbon through the holes so that the children can easily take the name strips off and put them on over their head.
5. Place a line of masking tape along the floor to indicate the stage area.
6. Pass out the nineteen tags in the order they appear in the story. The children without tags become the audience for the first performance.
7. Place "the child" on stage and read the story slowly. Children listen for their part and join "the child" on the stage (line).

NOTES:

Children need to be familiar with the order of the items to help them be ready for their part in the play.

A simple set of gray ears taped to a headband can be worn by Mouse.

If there is room on the tags children may draw a rebus.

Other books by Laura Joffe Numeroff include:
Emily's Bunch
Amy for Short

Other good stories to try this type of story theater with are:
  The Turnip, by Janina Domanska
  Drummer Hoff, by Barbara Emberley
  The Great Big Enormous Turnip, by Aleksei Tolstoi
  The Fat Cat, by Jack Kent

IF YOU GIVE A MOUSE A COOKIE

by Laura Numeroff

child
mouse
cookie
milk
straw
napkin
mirror
scissors
broom
box
blanket
pillow
story/favorite book
paper
crayons
picture
pen
scotch tape
refrigerator

Check It Out! The Book about Libraries

GAIL GIBBONS

(Harcourt Brace Jovanovich, 1985)

This informative book introduces modern library information centers. Simple explanations are colorfully presented, showing the history of libraries, public and school libraries, and the role of the librarian as a helper in finding answers to questions and in promoting reading. Call numbers are referred to as the "addresses" of library books.

PURPOSE:

Children explore the library and discover subjects of personal interest that can be located in a school or public library. Each child makes a bookmark listing subjects of personal interest.

MATERIALS:

(1) pattern for bookmark
Marking pens
Pencils
Scissors
Access to a school or public library

LET'S BEGIN:

1. Read *Check It Out! The Book about Libraries.*
2. Cut out the bookmark pattern.
3. Explore the library by looking at books and writing down subjects of interest.
4. List subjects you are interested in on the bookmark.
5. Color the top part of the bookmark.
6. Exchange bookmarks and notice the variety of subjects to be found in the books in the library.

NOTES:

This lesson may be used to introduce the subject catalog to children. To reinforce use of the subject catalog, cut pictures out of magazines and paste them on construction paper. Write the subject of each picture in capital letters above the picture. Examples: WHALES, DOGS, SPACE, BASEBALL, HALLOWEEN. Children can use these pictures to practice looking up subjects in the subject catalog.

Student bookmarks may be mounted on construction paper and laminated.

Related books:
    Tell Me Some More, by Crosby Bonsall
    Patrick Visits the Library, by Maureen Daly
    Quiet! There's a Canary in the Library, by Don Freeman
    I Like the Library, by Anne Rockwell

Our Snowman

M. B. GOFFSTEIN

(Harper & Row, 1986)

This story is about the wonderful memories of building a snowman. The simple illustrations depict a snowy world.

PURPOSE:

This art project allows children to recreate the pastel illustrations that M. B. Goffstein offers in this memorable story.

MATERIALS:

(1) 6x9-inch sheet of light green construction paper
White, black, brown colored chalks or pastels
Pencil
Ruler

LET'S BEGIN:

1. Read *Our Snowman*.
2. Discuss the type of art materials used to illustrate this book.
3. On the green paper draw a thin pencil frame similar to the pages in the book.
4. With the white chalk draw a snowman on the green paper.
5. Add details with the black and brown chalk.

NOTES:

Other books by M. B. Goffstein are:
  The Writer
  School of Names
  The Artist
  Fish for Supper

Related books are:
   The Snowman, by Raymond Briggs
   Kate's Snowman, by Kay Chorao
   Dear Snowman, by Janosch
   The Summer Snowman, by Gene Zion
   The First Snowfall, by Anne Rockwell and Harlow Rockwell
   Midnight Snowman, by Caroline Bauer

A similar art activity may be done with *The Chalk Box Story*, by Don Freeman.

The Snowman, by Raymond Briggs, is available on videotape (Snowman Enterprises Ltd., 1982), 26 minutes.

Bird's New Shoes

CHRIS RIDDELL

(Holt, 1987)

This story illustrates amusing aspects of fashion. Each animal is determined to be the best-dressed and most fashionable animal in the jungle. Buffalo, Anteater, Snake, Warthog, Rat, Goat, and Rabbit all get into the act until one of their friends brings them all back to reality.

PURPOSE:

Children enjoy an amusing story about fashion. They dress Bird in the latest fashion costume.

MATERIALS:

(1) pattern of Bird
Marking pens or crayons
Scissors
Feathers
(1) 12x18-inch piece of construction paper
Glue

LET'S BEGIN:

1. Read *Bird's New Shoes*.
2. Discuss "fashion" with children and how fashion changes.
3. Decorate Bird with marking pens or crayons, dressing Bird in the latest fashion.
4. Glue a feather on Bird.
5. Glue the bird you decorated to the right-hand side of the 12x18-inch piece of construction paper, which has been folded in half.
6. Cut the left-hand side of the paper as indicated in the illustration. Bird's head will show in the upper portion of your picture.
7. Share Bird's fashionable outfit with others in your class.

NOTES:

If you have access to magazines, let the children look through them for fashion ideas and pictures.

Related books:
The Emperor's New Clothes, by Hans Christian Andersen
I Like Old Clothes, by Mary Ann Hoberman
Jennie's Hat, by Ezra Jack Keats
The Seamstress of Salzburg, by Anita Lobel
The Case of the Sneaker Snatcher, by John Shearer

Boo!

BERNARD MOST

(Prentice-Hall, 1980)

The little monster is afraid of children. His monster "scares" never work. His monster friends tease him by wearing masks and pretending to be children. One day they leave behind a mask with a child's face on it. The little monster picks up the mask and puts it on. He stands in front of the mirror and scares himself for hours until he isn't afraid of children anymore.

PURPOSE:

In this activity children make a flip mask and recreate the events of the story.

MATERIALS:

(1) 8-inch square of blue paper
(1) 8-inch square of white paper
Pencils
Scissors
Paste or glue
Crayons or marking pens
Hole punch

LET'S BEGIN:

1. Read *Boo!*
2. Draw two 7-inch circles. Draw one circle on blue paper and one circle on white paper.
3. Cut out the two circles.
4. Make a fold horizontally on the white circle. The fold should be one-third of the way down from the top of the circle.
5. Paste or glue the top third of the white circle or the part above the fold to the top third of the blue circle.
6. Using black crayon or marking pen, color the blue circle to represent the monster in *Boo!* Include eyes, mouth, fangs, hairs, etc.
7. Color your own face on the white circle of paper. You now have your face mask on the front and can flip the bottom part up to see the monster's blue face.
8. Punch a hole in the right and left side of the attached circles and attach yarn strings.

NOTES:

Children might want to have a pointed head on the blue monster mask. Add the point with a scrap of blue paper.

Related books:
> *Dorrie and the Dreamyard Monsters*, by Patricia Coombs
> *Clyde Monster*, by Robert L. Crowe
> *Harry and the Terrible Whatzit*, by Dick Gackenbach
> *Four Scary Stories*, by Tony Johnston
> *Goodnight Orange Monster*, by Betty Jean Lifton
> *There's a Nightmare in My Closet*, by Mercer Mayer
> *Liza Lou and the Yeller Belly Swamp*, by Mercer Mayer
> *Zed and the Monsters*, by Peggy Parish
> *Where the Wild Things Are*, by Maurice Sendak
> "Could Be Worse," by James Stevenson
> *The Thing in Dolores' Piano*, by Robert Tallon
> *My Mama Says There Aren't Any Zombies, Ghosts, Vampires, Creatures, Demons, Monsters, Fiends, Goblins, or Things*, by Judith Viorst

For another monster activity, see *Creative Encounters: Activities to Expand Children's Responses to Literature*, by Anne T. Polkingharn and Catherine Toohey, p. 87: *There's a Nightmare in My Closet*, by Mercer Mayer

The Quilt Story

TONY JOHNSTON

(Putnam, 1985)

A quilt is lovingly made by a pioneer mother for her daughter and is discovered generations later in an attic by another little girl.

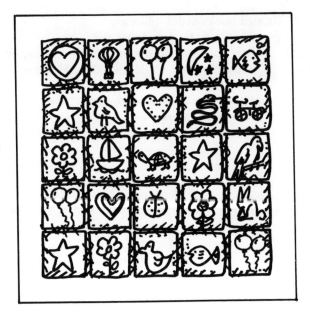

PURPOSE:

This activity allows each student to design and contribute a square to a class quilt.

MATERIALS:

(1) 8x8-inch piece of tagboard
Crayons or marking pens
Hole punch
Yarn
Large rug needles

LET'S BEGIN:

1. Read *The Quilt Story*.
2. Discuss the quilts, quilt designs, and patchwork quilts. Explain the history and variety of quilts.
3. Punch holes at 1-inch intervals along the sides of the tagboard.
4. Design and draw a quilt square on the tagboard with crayons or pens.
5. With the needle and yarn attach the individual squares with a simple crossover stitch.

NOTES:

Younger children will need the holes prepunched and assistance in stitching the pieces together.

The quilts can be done with a special theme (holiday, friendship, animals, families, etc.). This quilt makes an unusual hanging mural.

A future project would be to make a patchwork quilt with squares of muslin and permanent felt pens.

Related books about quilts are:
  The Quilt, by Ann Jonas
  Sam Johnson and the Blue Ribbon Quilt, by Lisa Campbell Ernst
  The Patchwork Quilt, by Valerie Hournoy

Other books by Tony Johnston and Tomie de Paola are:
  Four Scary Stories
  The Vanishing Pumpkin

Who Wants a Cheap Rhinoceros?

SHEL SILVERSTEIN

(Macmillan, 1983)

Who wants a cheap rhinoceros? I know of one for sale. The first page shows a FOR SALE sign. The content of the story tells the many helpful things a rhinoceros could do around your house.

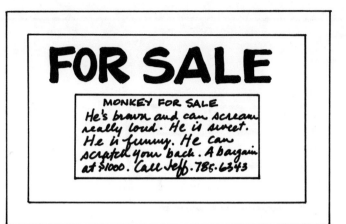

PURPOSE:

Children use the concept of a rhinoceros as helpful and extend this concept to think of another animal and how it might help in daily life. Using a FOR SALE sign, children write ways in which the animal of their choice might be helpful.

MATERIALS:

(1) FOR SALE sign
Marking pens
Pencils

LET'S BEGIN:

1. Read *Who Wants a Cheap Rhinoceros?*
2. Discuss how the rhinoceros was helpful in the story.
3. Give each child a FOR SALE sign.
4. Think of one animal and write its name on the front of the FOR SALE sign. Write your name and phone number and a price for your animal.
5. On the back of the FOR SALE sign, list ways that your animal might be helpful.
   Examples: A monkey could play on the jungle gym at recess.
   A parrot could help me learn my spelling words.
   A kangaroo could be useful as a backpack and carry my books and homework in his pouch.

NOTES:

This is a good time to introduce nonfiction animal books. These books will give children ideas for animals and animal characteristics.

Publishers of series of books on individual animals:
Raintree Children's Books. Example: *The Life Cycle of the Kangaroo*, by Paula Z. Hogan
Crestwood House. Example: *The Porcupine*, by Carl R. Green and William R. Sanford
Wildlife Education Ltd. Zoobooks. 42 separate titles about individual animals

Let's Make Rabbits

LEO LIONNI

(Pantheon, 1982)

This enjoyable fable begins with a pair of scissors and a pencil making rabbits. The adventure of the individual rabbits will delight students and teachers alike.

PURPOSE:

This project engages children in a collage project that emulates the unique style of Leo Lionni.

MATERIALS:

(2) 6x9-inch sheets of different wallpaper patterns
(1) 9x12-inch piece of colored construction paper
Patterns
Scissors
Glue
Scraps

LET'S BEGIN:

1. Select two sheets of wallpaper.
2. Number the sheets 1 and 2.
3. On the back of number 1 trace the corresponding pattern for the rabbit's body and ears.

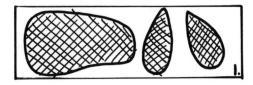

4. On the back of number 2 trace the pattern pieces for the rabbit's arms, legs, and head.

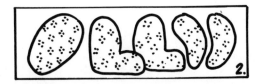

5. Cut out the pattern pieces.

41

6. Arrange the pattern pieces to represent a rabbit on the 9x12-inch colored paper.
7. When satisfied with the arrangement, glue the pieces onto the paper.
8. Add an eye, tail, background, and individual details (carrot, basket, eggs, etc.).

NOTES:

These colorful rabbits make a delightful bulletin board any time of the year. Cut out the words "Let's Make Rabbits" from wallpaper to accompany the pictures.

The Velveteen Rabbit is an appropriate book to read aloud after this project.

Other books to enjoy by Leo Lionni:
    Alexander and the Wind-up Mouse
    The Biggest House in the World
    Fish Is Fish
    Frederick
    Swimmy

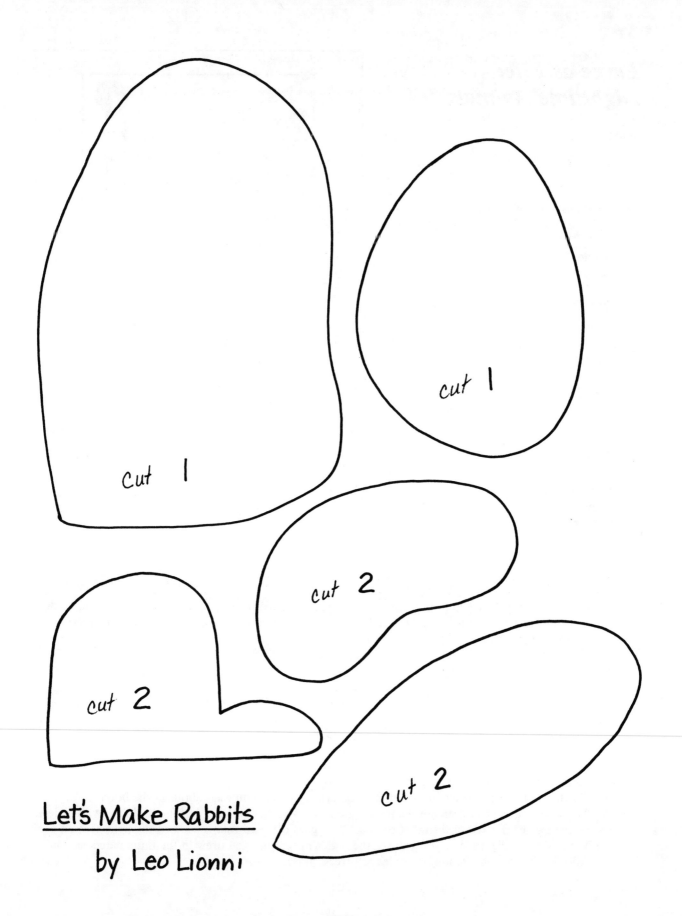

cut 1

cut 1

cut 2

cut 2

cut 2

Let's Make Rabbits

by Leo Lionni

43

Large as Life: Nighttime Animals

JOANNA COLE

(Knopf, 1985)

Nocturnal animals are featured in this book with brief text and paintings. The paintings of the animals are life size. Elf owls, a fennec fox, a chinchilla, a royal antelope, and giant toads are included.

PURPOSE:

Children make a "flashlight" picture showing an after-dark flashlight scene. In the beam of the flashlight one of the nighttime animals in the book is shown. The term "nocturnal animals" is reinforced.

MATERIALS:

(1) 9x12-inch medium blue paper
(1) 9x12-inch white paper
Glue
Pencils
Scissors
Marking pens and crayons
Stapler
Clear plastic tape

LET'S BEGIN:

1. Read *Large as Life: Nighttime Animals*.
2. On the 9x12-inch medium blue construction paper placed horizontally, draw a nighttime flashlight scene in which you are holding the flashlight and standing to one side of the paper directing a triangular beam of light toward the other side of the paper.
3. When this picture has been completed, cut out the "light" or blue triangular piece.

4. Glue the medium blue paper to the white paper.
5. On the white section draw in one of the nocturnal animals you read about in the book.
6. The blue cutaway piece can now be put to good use. Attach it at the end of the flashlight with a piece of clear tape. Fold it forward so that the flashlight goes off, and fold it back so the light goes on again. When the flashlight is on, you will see the nighttime animal you drew in the illuminated section.
7. Add details such as a moon, stars, leaves, trees, grass, etc.

NOTES:

This idea was adapted from a book of art ideas by Gene Baer, *Wild and Wonderful Art Lessons*, Parker, 1983.

The companion volume to *Large as Life: Nighttime Animals* is *Large as Life: Daytime Animals*, by Joanna Cole.

Related books:
How Animals Sleep, by Millicent Selsam
Night Animals, by Millicent Selsam
Exploring the Midnight World, by Christopher Tunney
Creatures of the Night, by Judith E. Rinard

Miss Nelson Is Missing!

HARRY ALLARD

(Houghton Mifflin, 1971)

This is a story of a noisy class of children in Room 209 and their teacher, Miss Nelson. Miss Nelson engages the assistance of Miss Viola Swamp to creatively solve the problem of the unruly students in Room 209.

PURPOSE:

Children will write imaginative stories about the whereabouts of their teacher when someone plays the role of a substitute teacher.

MATERIALS:

Writing paper or lined tagboard
Pencils

LET'S BEGIN:

1. Read *Miss Nelson Is Missing!* prior to this activity.
2. Make plans with another teacher to trade classes for the first period of the morning.
3. On the appointed morning, each teacher needs to stay hidden from his/her own class.
4. Have a secretary, principal, or volunteer take the substitute teacher to the designated classroom and announce that Ms./Mr. _____ is here to substitute for Ms./Mr. _____ because Ms./Mr. _____ is missing.
5. Allow students time to discuss the strangeness of the absence and possible explanations.
6. Some children may realize that it is like the book *Miss Nelson Is Missing!* Let children recall what the students in Room 209 thought of after Miss Nelson disappeared.
7. Think of other "fantastic" things that could have happened to the missing teacher.
8. Write these adventures and remember to include an introduction and conclusion to the mysterious absence.
9. Share the stories with the class.
10. The substitute teachers may return to their original classes. Students may read the stories of "Ms./Mr. _____ Is Missing!"

NOTES:

Younger children may need to be reassured that this is similar to the book of *Miss Nelson Is Missing!*

This can be a language experience activity with younger children.

Other books by Harry Allard include:
Miss Nelson Is Back
Miss Nelson Has a Field Day
There's a Party at Mona's Tonight

James Marshall has illustrated Harry Allard's books and also collaborated on:
The Stupids Die
The Stupids Step Out
The Stupids Have a Ball

Father Time and the Day Boxes

GEORGE ELLA LYON

(Bradbury, 1985)

This book describes how each day comes to us. Father Time works in a Time Vault. Every twenty-four hours he throws down a day box, inviting us to help ourselves to a day. He reminds us, "You can't come back for seconds."

PURPOSE:

Children talk about the concept of time including facts relating to calendars and time while constructing a day box from the pattern provided.

MATERIALS:

(1) pattern for a day box
Scissors
Cellophane tape
Pencils
Marking pens

LET'S BEGIN:

1. Read *Father Time and the Day Boxes*.
2. Cut out the day box using the pattern provided.
3. Discuss time, measurement, and concepts of time using facts about clocks and calendars.
4. Write facts about time on the chalkboard.
   Examples: There are 365 days in one year.
   There are 24 hours in one day.
   There are 7 days in one week.
   There are 60 minutes on one hour.
   There are 60 seconds in one minute.
   The sundial, water glass, hourglass, and clock all measure time. Clocks in different parts of the world do not all have the same time.
5. Write a different fact about time on each side of the day box pattern.
6. Cut, fold, and tape together the day box.
7. Decorate the day box with marking pens.

NOTES:

Related books:

Mary Alice, Operator Number 9, by Jeffrey Allen
All Kinds of Time, by Harry Behn
The Grouchy Ladybug, by Eric Carle
Clocks and More Clocks, by Pat Hutchins
When Is Tomorrow?, by Nancy Dingman Watson
The True Book of Time, by Feenie Ziner and Elizabeth Thompson
Over and Over, by Charlotte Zolotow

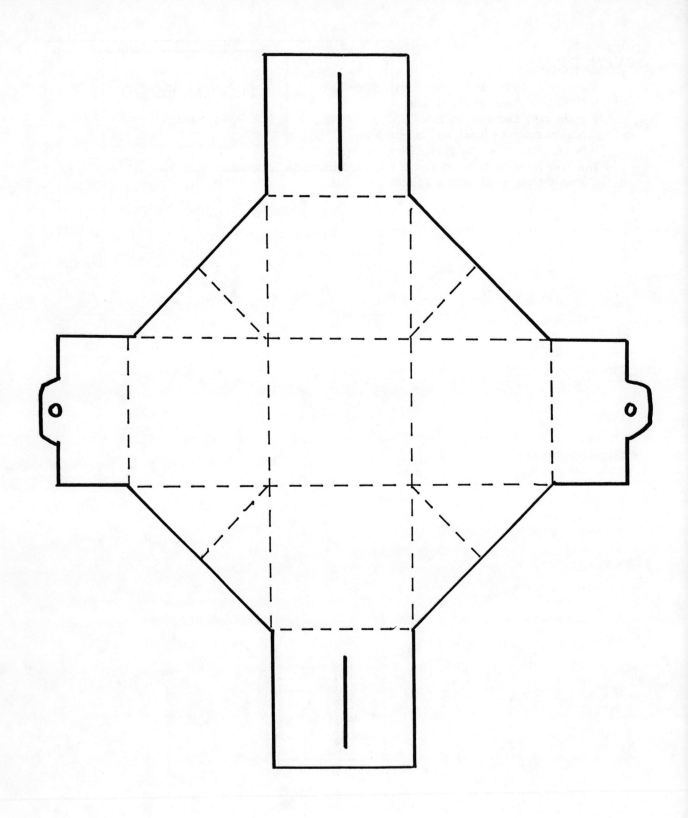

Seven Eggs

MEREDITH HOOPER

(Harper & Row, 1985)

On each day of the week a different egg hatches. What hatches from each egg informs and delights the reader.

PURPOSE:

In this project children follow the format of the book to reinforce the days of the week and the concept that some animals hatch from eggs.

MATERIALS:

(3) 6x11-inch sheets of white paper
(2) 6x20-inch sheets
Long-arm stapler
Pencils
Crayons or marking pens
Small piece of foil

LET'S BEGIN:

1. Read *Seven Eggs*.
2. Take three sheets of 6x11-inch paper and layer it with 1½-inch overlaps on the right-hand side.
3. Fold the paper over toward the right side to double the number of overlapped pages.

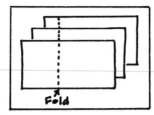

4. Fold 6x20-inch sheets in half to form a cover and first page for the overlap pages.
5. On the inside front cover write, "There were seven eggs."

6. Beginning on the inside of the smallest flap, write the days of the week starting with Monday.

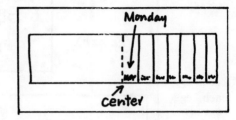

7. On each overlap let children draw an egg. Each egg may vary in size.
8. Draw an animal on each page that could hatch from the drawn egg.
9. On the Sunday page glue the foil shape to represent the chocolate egg that was eaten.

NOTES:

This is a lengthy project and should be done in steps to avoid confusion and rushing.

There are many nonfiction books that teach more understanding about eggs.
Chickens Aren't the Only Ones, by Ruth Heller
Egg to Chick, by Millicent E. Selsam
What's Hatching Out of That Egg?, by Patricia Lauber

Another book to read to reinforce the days of the week:
The Very Hungry Caterpillar, by Eric Carle

The Little Old Lady Who Was Not Afraid of Anything

LINDA WILLIAMS

(Crowell, 1986)

One dark autumn night the little old lady who was not afraid of anything gets the SCARE of her life. The little old lady confronts a pumpkin head, two big shoes, a pair of pants, a silly shirt, a pair of gloves, and a tall black hat. She whispers an idea in the pumpkin's ear and is surprised the next morning.

PURPOSE:

Children color, cut, and assemble the scary parts that the old lady meets. They construct the scarecrow that appears at the end of the story.

MATERIALS:

(1) copy of scarecrow pattern
Marking pens or crayons
Scissors
(3) brads

LET'S BEGIN:

1. Read *The Little Old Lady Who Was Not Afraid of Anything.*
2. Using the pattern parts provided, color each part that scared the little old lady.
3. Cut out the pattern pieces after coloring them.
4. Attach the pattern pieces with brads to form the scarecrow that surprised the little old lady when she woke up the next morning and looked out into her garden.

NOTES:

This is a good story to read in the fall, but it is not necessarily a Halloween story.

A similar activity can be found in *Creative Encounters*, p. 37, *The Bump in the Night*, by Anne Rockwell.

Related books:
Joji and the Dragon, by Betty Jean Lifton
The Strawman Who Smiled by Mistake, by Paul Tripp
The Night the Scarecrow Walked, by Natalie Savage Carlson

Darkness and the Butterfly

ANN GRIFALCONI

(Little, Brown, 1987)

This beautifully illustrated book captures the universal fear of darkness through an African child's eyes.

PURPOSE:

This activity involves making a special butterfly and talking about the individual fears of darkness.

MATERIALS:

(1) butterfly pattern
(1) 9x12-inch piece of white construction paper
Yellow poster paint
(1) 9x12-inch piece of dark blue construction paper

LET'S BEGIN:

1. Read *Darkness and the Butterfly*.
2. Fold the white sheet of paper in half. After creasing the paper, unfold it.

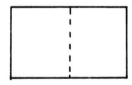

3. Put several blobs of yellow paint on one half of the paper.

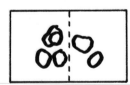

4. Refold the paper and press over the paper to smear the yellow paint.
5. Allow paint to dry.

6. Fold and trace butterfly pattern.

7. Cut and glue onto dark blue paper.
8. Cut stars from yellow scraps and glue onto the blue paper.

NOTES:

Other books by Ann Grifalconi include:
  Village of Round and Square Houses
  The Toy Trumpet

Related books that discuss children's fears in universal ways are:
  Who's Afraid of the Dark?, by Crosby Bonsall
  Frizzy the Fearful, by Marjorie Weinman Sharmat
  Chin Chiang and the Dragon's Dance, by Ian Wallace

This project easily lends itself to a class mural activity.

Clyde Monster

ROBERT L. CROWE

(Dutton, 1976)

Clyde is a little monster with an unusual problem. He is afraid of people. His parents help him overcome his fear in a way that all children and monsters will enjoy.

PURPOSE:

This activity involves making a cave that opens and helps children discuss their fears.

MATERIALS:

(1) 9x12-inch piece of light brown construction paper
(1) 6x9-inch piece of white construction paper
Crayons or marking pens

LET'S BEGIN:

1. Read *Clyde Monster*.
2. Tear around the brown construction paper to achieve a bumpy cave outline.

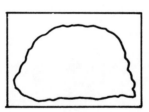

3. Tear a door into the cave.

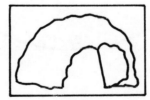

4. On the back of the door glue the white sheet of paper.
5. Draw a monster on the white sheet of paper. When the door opens, he will be peeking fearfully from the cave opening.

NOTES:

This is an excellent accompaniment to *There's a Nightmare in My Closet*, by Mercer Mayer.

Other books to read about monster's fears are:
    Boo!, by Bernard Most
    My Mama Says There Aren't Any Zombies, Ghosts, Vampires, Creatures, Demons, Monsters, Fiends,
        Goblins, or Things, by Judith Viorst

The Magic School Bus at the Waterworks

JOANNA COLE

(Scholastic Book Services, 1986)

Ms. Frizzle takes her class on a field trip to the waterworks, where she parks the school bus on a cloud and everyone, even "the Friz," shrinks to raindrop size. The class members see the waterworks from the water's point of view as they travel through the city waterworks.

PURPOSE:

Children review the sequence of events in the story as they learn how water gets into the faucets in our homes. Each child makes a raindrop-shaped booklet, writing and reviewing the sequence of the events presented in the book. Children learn about the purification of water.

MATERIALS:

(11) sheets of lined paper cut in raindrop shape (see pattern)
(1) piece of plain white paper for the cover of the booklet cut in raindrop shape
Pencils and marking pens
Scissors
Stapler

LET'S BEGIN:

1. Read *The Magic School Bus at the Waterworks*.
2. Take time to talk about the detailed drawings in the story, the notes from the author (for serious students only) on pages 38 and 39, and look carefully at Ms. Frizzle's wardrobe (theme dresses and shoes). Explain that the waterworks system in your town may differ slightly from the waterworks described in the book.
3. To make the booklet, each child will need a raindrop cover and 11 pieces of lined paper cut into the raindrop shape. Number your lined paper from 1 to 11.
4. Looking at pages 34 and 35, the teacher writes each numbered fact on the chalkboard. Children copy one fact on each of the eleven sheets of lined raindrop-shaped paper. Each child will have eleven steps. Children illustrate each step.
5. To make the cover, each child draws a picture of himself or herself in the raindrop. Be sure to include a mask, snorkel, fins, and bathing suit.
6. Staple the cover on the front of the booklet.
7. Put the title *The Magic School Bus at the Waterworks* on the cover.

NOTES:

Call or write to your local waterworks for information, and compare the procedure for water purification in your town with the one in the book. The water department may be willing to come to your school and give a water conservation program.

See the book *The Magic School Bus inside the Earth*, by Joanna Cole, in which Ms. Frizzle makes earth science an adventure when she takes her students to the center of the earth.

Related books:
    From Ice to Rain, by Marlene Reidel
    Water, by Carme Vendrell
    Liquid Magic, by Philip Watson

Books by Joanna Cole:
    Bony-Legs. Four Winds, 1983.
    Doctor Change. Morrow, 1986.
    Large as Life, Daytime Animals. Knopf, 1985.
    Large as Life, Nighttime Animals. Knopf, 1985.
    The *Laugh Book*. Doubleday, 1986.
    The Secret Box. Morrow, 1971.

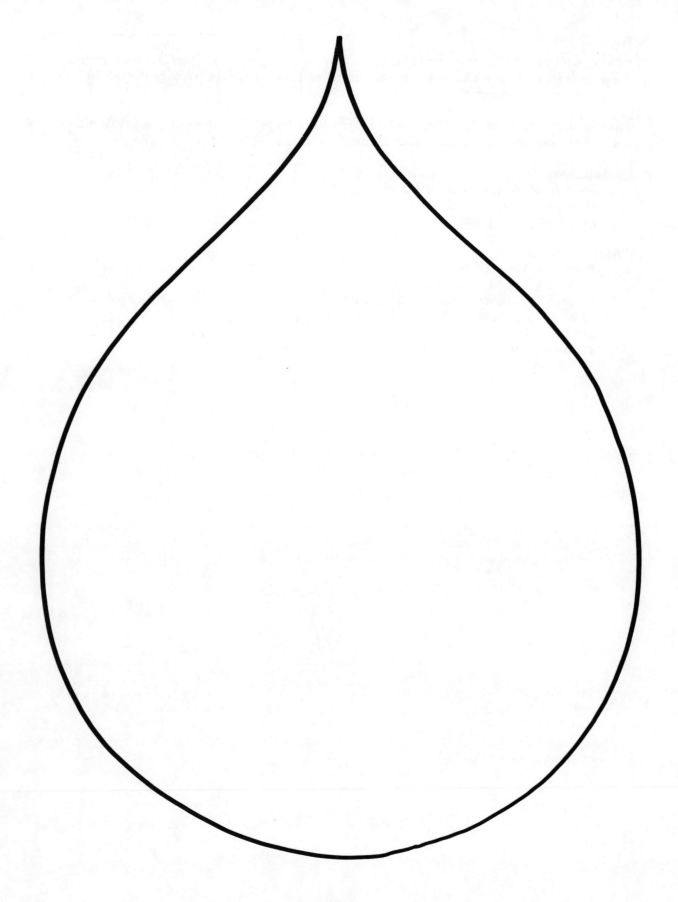

Golly Gump Swallowed a Fly

JOANNA COLE

(Crown, 1987)

Golly Gump wins a yawning contest. As he recalls the contest he swallows a fly and continues swallowing animals until the humorous conclusion.

PURPOSE:

In this activity children contribute to a large class mural of Golly Gump.

MATERIALS:

(2) large sheets of white butcher paper
(1) 6x9-inch piece of white construction paper
Marking pens or crayons
Scissors
Glue

LET'S BEGIN:

1. Read *Golly Gump Swallowed a Fly*.
2. Draw a large outline of the fat Golly Gump on the butcher paper. You may use an overhead projector.
3. Lay the outline of Golly Gump on another large sheet of the butcher paper and cut around both sheets.
4. Fill in the details of Golly Gump's face and clothing. Glue the top paper with Golly Gump onto the other sheet so that Golly Gump is attached at the head and shoulders.
5. On the 6x9-inch sheet of paper draw one of the characters that Golly Gump swallowed.

6. Color and cut out the characters.
7. Lift the clothing section of Golly Gump (top sheet), and glue the characters onto the "inside of his stomach."
8. Place the mural on the bulletin board so that the children may lift Golly Gump's clothing to see everything he swallowed.

NOTES:

Read and sing "I Know an Old Lady Who Swallowed a Fly." Other books by Joanna Cole are listed on page 61.

The Rebus Treasury

JEAN MARZOLLO, compiler

(Dial, 1986)

A rebus is simply a picture substituted for a word's sound or meaning. Forty-one favorite songs and rhymes are collected in full-color rebuses in this treasury.

MATERIALS:

(1) piece of lined paper
(1) pattern rebus page
Pencil
Marking pens
Glue
Scissors

LET'S BEGIN:

1. Read selections from *The Rebus Treasury*. Show the rebus as a picture substituted for a word's sound or meaning.
2. Cut out the rebus squares on the pattern page.
3. Create your own sentences using the rebus squares as substitutes for a word's sound or meaning.
4. Use lined paper and glue the rebus squares in the appropriate places in your written sentences.
5. Color the pictures in the rebus squares.
6. Share your sentences with others in the class.

NOTES:

The rebus pattern sheet includes these words: Left-hand column: bells, ring, love, hen, can. Right-hand column: stars, world, eye, you, hat.

Other rebus books:
   The Little Red Riding Hood Rebus Book, retold by Ann Morris (includes a rebus dictionary)
   Mother Goose Picture Riddles: A Book of Rebuses, by Lisl Weil
   Bunny Rabbit Rebus, by David A. Adler

Old Henry

JOAN W. BLOS

(Morrow, 1987)

Old Henry seemingly does nothing to improve his neighborhood. His neighbors force him to move. In the end they miss each others' eccentric ways.

PURPOSE:

In this activity children respond to Henry's letter with a personal letter from the mayor.

MATERIALS:

(1) piece of lined notebook paper
Pencil or pen

LET'S BEGIN:

1. Read *Old Henry*.
2. The last page of the book invites an answer to Henry's letter.
3. Consider different responses the mayor could write to Henry.
4. On notebook paper similar to Henry's, draft a letter to Henry from the mayor.
5. Share your letters.

NOTES:

Select other members of the town who could have answered Henry's letter.

Other books by Joan Blos include the 1980 Newbery Medal winner, *A Gathering of Days*, and *Martin's Hats*.

Stephen Gammel's beautiful illustrations enhance this book. He also illustrated two Caldecott Honor Books, *Where the Buffaloes Begin*, by Olaf Baker, and *The Relatives Came*, by Cynthia Rylant.

Mrs. Dunphy's Dog

CATHARINE O'NEILL

(Viking Kestrel, 1987)

Every evening James, the dog, and Mrs. Dunphy stroll to the newsstand to pick up Mrs. Dunphy's newspaper. When James reads the headlines, he is stunned. He doesn't know how he learned to read. James keeps eating up the news and discovering new headlines and books to devour.

PURPOSE:

Children read a newspaper or *My Weekly Reader* and cut out an article or paragraph that would be interesting to James.

MATERIALS:

(1) pattern of James the dog
Marking pens
Copies of *My Weekly Reader* or other current newspapers or magazines
Scissors
Glue

LET'S BEGIN:

1. Read *Mrs. Dunphy's Dog*.
2. Pass out newspapers, magazines, or copies of *My Weekly Reader*.
3. Read the newspaper, magazine, or *My Weekly Reader* to find an article of interest.
4. Cut out an article that you enjoyed.
5. Glue the article in the square on the pattern page for James to read.
6. Share your article by reading it to the rest of the class.

NOTES:

Related books:
> *Louis James Hates School*, by Bill Morrison
> *When Will I Read?*, by Miriam Cohen
> *I Can Read with My Eyes Shut*, by Dr. Seuss
> *Today Was a Terrible Day*, by Patricia Giff
> *Arthur's Prize Reader*, by Lillian Hoban
> *Broderick*, by Edward Ormondroyd

MRs. DUNPHY'S DOG
by Catharine O'Neill

What a Catastrophe!

WAYNE CAMPBELL

(Bradbury, 1986)

A humorous story about a frog's adventures at a family's breakfast table. This story has several different endings.

Ending 5

My frog landed in Mom's cereal bowl. Boy was she mad. She picked him up with her spoon and put him in the garden.

PURPOSE:

This writing activity encourages independent thinking and creative writing. Each child writes an imaginative ending to the story.

MATERIALS:

Writing paper
Pencil or pen

LET'S BEGIN:

1. Read *What a Catastrophe!* Stop on the page where the boy asks, "What could have happened to it?"
2. Elicit and write on the chalkboard words children might need to make up an ending to the story.
3. The author wrote four endings for this catastrophe. Encourage students to write new ones.
4. Share the students' endings and then read the four endings the author wrote.
5. Compare the variety of endings.

NOTES:

This is a good prelude to an interactive fiction series.

The songbook, *The Foolish Frog*, by Pete Seeger, is a good accompaniment to this book.

Related books about frogs:
  Seven Froggies Went to School, by Kate Duke
  The Mysterious Tadpole, by Steven Kellogg
  A Boy, a Dog, a Frog and a Friend, by Mercer Mayer

Other problem-solving books include:
  What Do You Do with a Kangaroo, by Mercer Mayer
  It Could Always Be Worse, by Margot Zemach

The Paper Crane

MOLLY BANG

(Greenwillow, 1985)

A mysterious man appears at a restaurant, hungry but penniless. The owner feeds him and is rewarded by a gift from the man. The gift is a paper napkin folded into a crane which comes to life at the clap of a hand. Three-dimensional illustrations enhance this book.

PURPOSE:

Children review the story and cut and fold a paper crane.

MATERIALS:

(1) crane pattern page
(1) 12x18-inch piece of construction paper
Scissors
Marking pens or crayons
Glue

LET'S BEGIN:

1. Read *The Paper Crane*.
2. Fold the construction paper in half.
3. Place the bird pattern with its fold line on the folded edge of the piece of construction paper.
4. Trace the bird pattern and cut it out.
5. Color the bird.
6. Cut a slit in the construction paper bird as marked on the pattern.
7. Take the tip of each wing and pull the wing tip through the slit on each side of the body.
8. Add paper legs to the bird.

NOTES:

This crane pattern works well in a group situation where it is difficult to teach origami paper folding to younger children. For older children look up a folded origami bird or crane pattern in one of the origami books listed below.

Related books:
   Japan's Creative Origami, by Toyoaki Kawai
   Easy Origami, by Dokuohtei Nakano
   Origami in the Classroom (2 volumes), by Chiyo Araki

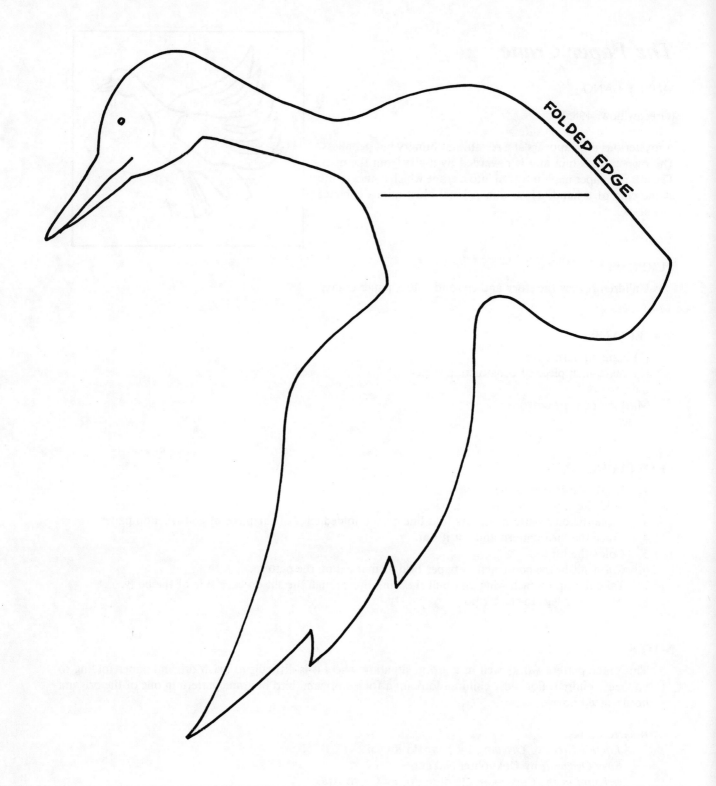

FOLDED EDGE

The Mitten

ALVIN TRESSELT

(Scholastic Book Services, 1985)

This is a traditional Russian folktale about a small boy who loses his mitten and the melange of animals that inhabit the lost mitten.

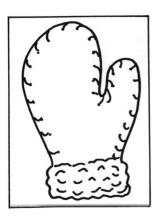

PURPOSE:

In this project children make a mtiten to help retell the events from the folktale.

MATERIALS:

(1) copy of mitten pattern
(2) 9x12-inch sheet of white construction paper
(1) 36-inch piece of yarn
(1) large rug needle
Crayons or marking pens
Furlike material or cotton

LET'S BEGIN:

1. Read *The Mitten*.
2. Fold the white paper in half.
3. Trace the mitten pattern onto the white folded paper.

4. Cut out the mitten.
5. Color the outside of the mitten halves.
6. Thread the needle with the yarn and stitch the mitten together.

7. Fold the second sheet of construction paper in sixths (first in half and then thirds). In the sections draw the following: (1) mouse and frog, (2) owl and rabbit, (3) fox, (4) wolf, (5) boar, (6) bear. Cricket can be drawn on any of the sections.

8. Color the animals and cut them out.
9. Glue the fur or cotton along the opening of the mitten.
10. Place the animals in the mitten, recalling the details from the story.

NOTES:

To help draw the animals use Ed Emberley's *Drawing Book of Animals.*

This is a very good cooperative activity. Divide the children into groups of four. Make a larger mitten pattern and let each child draw two of the animals. The cricket will need to be drawn also.

This activity makes a winter bulletin board with lots of colorful mittens lying in the snow.

Related books about mittens:
    Too Many Mittens, by Florence and Louis Slobodkin
    Mittens in May, by Maxine Kumin
    The Mystery of the Missing Red Mitten, by Steven Kellogg

Younger children may need holes punched in their mittens to facilitate the sewing.

Imogene's Antlers

DAVID SMALL

(Crown, 1985)

When Imogene awakens, she discovers she has grown antlers. The family doctor, the school principal, the local milliner, and even her brother fail to resolve this dilemma. The problem appears solved when Imogene awakes antler-free the next morning—but readers are in for a surprise ending.

PURPOSE:

Children imagine themselves in Imogene's predicament as they decorate the pattern page to represent themselves wearing antlers.

MATERIALS:

(1) Imogene's antlers pattern page
Crayons and marking pens

LET'S BEGIN:

1. Read *Imogene's Antlers*.
2. Draw your face on the Imogene's antlers pattern and color your antlers.
3. Decorate the antlers with donuts, birds, Christmas ornaments, or other decorations.

NOTES:

Imagine other animal parts Imogene might have grown and how she would have looked. Examples: elephant's trunk, giraffe's neck, duck feet, kangaroo pouch, etc.

Related books:
  Mother Rabbit's Son Tom, by Dick Gackenbach
  Carrot Nose, by Jan Wahl
  It's Not Easy Being a Bunny, by Marilyn Sadler
  Just So Stories, by Rudyard Kipling
  Buford the Little Bighorn, by Bill Peet
  I Wish That I Had Duck Feet, by Theo LeSieg

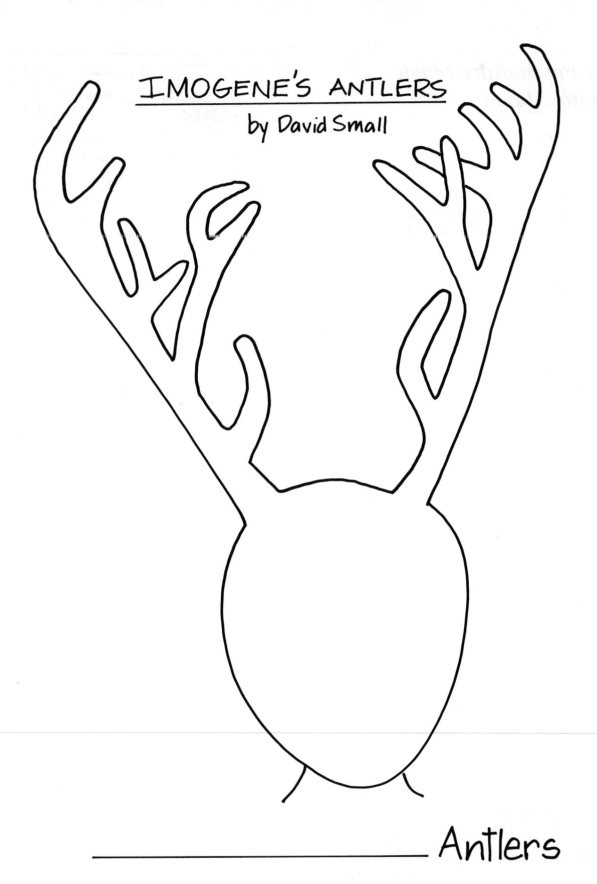

IMOGENE'S ANTLERS
by David Small

_____ Antlers

Pig Pig and the Magic Photo Album

DAVID McPHAIL

(Dutton, 1986)

Pig Pig is waiting to have his picture taken at the photographer's. Magically, every time Pig Pig says the word "cheese" while flipping through a photo album he encounters many adventures.

Cheese, Pig Pig found himself in a witch's caldron.

PURPOSE:

In this activity children create an additional adventure for Pig Pig by following the theme of the book. Children write individual adventures for a photo album.

MATERIALS:

(1) 12x18-inch piece of black construction paper
(1) 8x8-inch sheet of white paper
(1) 8½x11-inch sheet of writing paper
(4) art corners
Crayons or marking pens

LET'S BEGIN:

1. Read *Pig Pig and the Magic Photo Album*.
2. Think of a further adventure in which Pig Pig could find himself.
3. Thinking of an adventure, list some of the words you might need to incorporate in Pig Pig's adventure.
4. Write about Pig Pig's next adventure. Be certain to begin your story with "cheese."
5. Illustrate the story on the white square.
6. Fold the black paper in half.
7. With the four art corners put the picture in place on the left side of the fold.
8. Glue the final version of your story on the right side of the fold.
9. Share the stories.

NOTES:

Enjoy these books by David McPhail:
Pig Pig Rides
Pig Pig Goes to Camp
Pig Pig Grows Up
Fix-it
The Dream Child
Emma's Pet
Emma's Vacation

These projects could be put into a class photo album.

Paper John

DAVID SMALL

(Farrar, Straus & Giroux, 1987)

Young John makes his living selling paper toys, flowers, kites, and favors. He wears a paper hat, sleeps in a paper bed; even his house is made of paper. When an angry imposter has the whole town blown out to sea, Paper John refolds his house into a boat and sails to the rescue.

PURPOSE:

This story is a natural for origami activities, especially the transformation of a house to a boat. Learning to fold a newspaper boat for Paper John is an activity younger children can practice at school and enjoy doing at home.

MATERIALS:

(1) 14-inch square piece of newspaper
(1) pattern directions for folding the newspaper boat
Construction paper scraps

LET'S BEGIN:

1. Read *Paper John*.
2. Pass out the squares of newspaper.
3. Follow the directions and fold a newspaper boat.
4. Cut Young John and any of the townsfolk out of construction paper and place them in the fold of the boat.

NOTES:

Children might like to cut out or draw the gray demon.

Related books:
  Easy Origami, by Dokuohtei Nakano
  Origami in the Classroom (2 volumes), by Chiyo Araki
  Paperfolding for Beginners, by William D. Murray and Francis Rigney
  ABCs of Origami, by Claude Sarasas

PAPER JOHN
by David Small

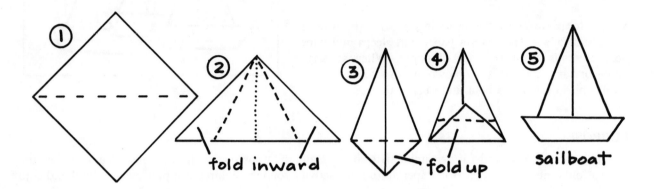

①

②
fold inward

③

④
fold up

⑤
sailboat

SAILBOAT (1) Start by folding a 14" square piece of newspaper in half to make a triangle. (2) Now fold the sides of the triangle up and inward to meet at a vertical center line. (3) The points at the bottom of this figure are folded up (4), and one final upward fold (5) gives you a nice sailboat.

Hattie and the Fox

MEM FOX

(Bradbury, 1987)

In this cumulative tale, Hattie the hen spots a fox in the bushes. Each of the other story characters is very apathetic about the fox until the very end of the story.

PURPOSE:

This activity allows children the opportunity to dramatize the story.

MATERIALS:

(7) 11x6-inch strips of paper
Yarn
Hole punch
Marking pen

LET'S BEGIN:

1. Read *Hattie and the Fox*.
2. Prepare strips with comments that each animal in the book typically makes:

    "Good Grief!" (Goose)
    "Well, well!" (Pig)
    "Who cares?" (Sheep)
    "So what?" (Horse)
    "What next?" (Cow)

3. On the reverse side of each character's card write the quote he or she says at the end of the story:

   "Oh, no!" (Goose)
   "Dear me!" (Pig)
   "Oh, dear!" (Sheep)
   "Oh, help!" (Horse)
   "Moo!" (Cow)
4. On the two remaining tags, write "Hattie" and "Fox."
5. Punch holes and string yarn to fit over each character's head.
6. Assign seven students a part by handing them a tag to put over their head.
7. Place a strip of masking tape on the floor to designate a stage line.
8. Reread the story and let the individual characters recite their lines. They can turn their tags over at the end to show the animals' change in attitude.
9. Save the tags and reread the story so that all children may have an opportunity to be an animal or the audience.

NOTES:

This is a good story to compare with *The Little Red Hen*.

The illustrations were done by Patricia Mullins with tissue paper and crayon. Children may enjoy making their own paper animals with tissue paper, crayons, and starch.

Other books by Mem Fox include:
   Arabella: The Smallest Girl in the World
   Possum Magic
   Wilfrid Gordon McDonald Partridge

Humphrey the Lost Whale: A True Story

WENDY TOKUDA AND RICHARD HALL

(Heian International, Inc., 1986)

The authors of this book work for a television station and helped to cover the story of Humphrey the whale on "Eye Witness News" in the San Francisco area. Humphrey, a humpback whale, wanders under the Golden Gate Bridge into San Francisco Bay. Instead of swimming back out to sea, he swims the wrong way up the Sacramento River. This book is the true story of how Humphrey's friends saved his life.

PURPOSE:

In this activity children construct a class bulletin board or mural depicting the journey of Humphrey, using a map of the San Francisco Bay area and three-dimensional paper whales.

MATERIALS:

(1) copy of whale pattern
Scissors
Marking pens
Clear adhesive tape
Light blue or white background paper for a class mural. The background paper may be 4x4-feet or larger if you have the bulletin board space.

LET'S BEGIN:

1. Read *Humphrey the Lost Whale: A True Story*.
2. Using the inside cover of the book as a guide and the piece of background paper, draw a map of the Pacific Ocean, Golden Gate Bridge (in red), San Pablo Bay area, Bay Bridge, Sacramento River, and Shag Slough.
3. Explain to the children where California is, using the inset map on the inside cover of the book or a larger map of the United States.
4. Assign one child to make Humphrey the humpback whale. Using the whale pattern, cut and fold and tape Humphrey. Put a capital H on Humphrey's back. (Cut on solid lines, fold on dotted lines.)
5. The other children make and fold humpback whales to be placed in the ocean and in San Francisco Bay in groups, or pods.
6. Place the folded paper Humphrey on the wall mural far away from the rest of the whales. Place Humphrey in the Sacramento River area or Shag Slough.

NOTES:

Humphrey tried to find his way back to the ocean for 26 days. More than 500 people and $80,000 were involved in the rescue effort.

Ask the children to think of methods they might have used to lure Humphrey back into the ocean.

Another television news event made into a children's book is *A Moose for Jessica*, by Pat Wakefield and Larry Carrara.

Another book about Humphrey is *Humphrey the Wayward Whale* by Ernest Callenbach and Christine Leefeldt. Heyday Books, Berkeley, Calif.

Related books:
Whale Watch, by June Behrens
The Humpback Whale, by Carl R. Green
When the Whale Came to my Town, by Jim Young
A Year in the Life of a Whale, by John Stidworthy and Jean Colville

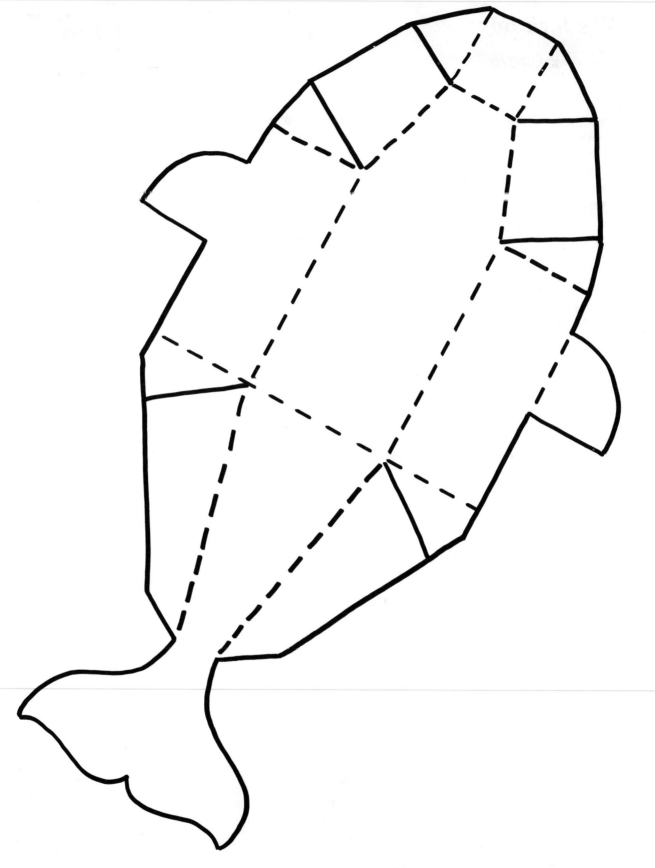

85

The Inch Boy

JUNKO MORIMOTO

(Viking Kestrel, 1984)

This is a traditional Japanese folktale about the heroic adventures of Issunboshi. Issunboshi, only one inch tall, sets out from his parents' home to see the world. In his adventures he meets a lovely princess and conquers a red demon.

PURPOSE:

In this project children make a one-inch boy and appreciate the Japanese fairy tale. Children will understand how small the brave and adventurous Issunboshi is.

MATERIALS:

(1) 1-inch square of white paper
Pen or thin marking pens
Glue

LET'S BEGIN:

1. Read *The Inch Boy*.
2. Draw a one-inch figure on the square.
3. Add details from the story (kimono, soup bowl, chopsticks, etc.)
4. Glue each one-inch figure onto a larger sheet of paper to form a class mural of Issunboshis.

NOTES:

This is an excellent story to compare and contrast with the European folktale of *Tom Thumb*.

Locate Japan on the globe for the children.

Other Japanese tales for young children include:
The Stonecutter, by Gerald McDermott
The Crane Maiden, by Miyoko Matsutami
The Funny Little Woman, by Arlene Mosel
Peach Boy and Other Japanese Children's Favorite Stories, by Florence Skade

This project is simple but effective because children are often used to standard paper sizes.

For creative writing children can glue their one-inch figures on a sheet of writing paper and write another adventure for Issunboshi.

Claude and Sun

MATT NOVAK

(Bradbury, 1987)

This story relates the importance of the sun and sunlight to man. The impressionistic art imitates the style of Van Gogh.

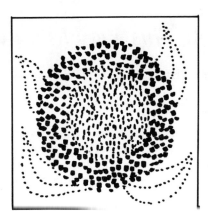

PURPOSE:

This art project allows children to study impressionism by drawing a small picture using the method of great artists.

MATERIALS:

(1) 6x6-inch square piece of white construction paper
Crayons

LET'S BEGIN:

1. Read *Claude and Sun*.
2. Discuss art techniques used by impressionists.
3. Using only small dots of color draw a sunflower or sun on the white square.
4. Using the same dot technique color the background space.

NOTES:

Another technique for beginning pointillism is dipping a cotton swab in poster paint and dotting the paint on the paper.

Related books about art:
   Linnea in Monet's Garden, by Christina Björak; illustrated by Lena Anderson
   An Artist's Album, by M. B. Goffstein
   The Sun, by Seymour Simon, is an information book about the sun.

Another book by Matt Novak is *Rolling*.

At This Very Minute

KATHLEEN RICE BOWERS

(Little, Brown, 1983)

This unusual bedtime story shows activities taking place all over the world as the child is ready for bed. "At this very minute," people watch television, a baby is taking its first look, a family has just arrived from a faraway land, and a grandmother is sitting waiting for the phone to ring.

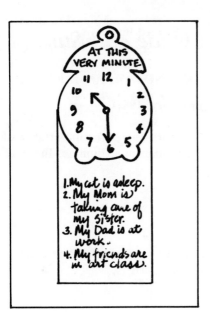

PURPOSE:

Children think of events happening in the world around them. They imagine events that might be happening around the world "at this very minute" and write these events on a clock.

MATERIALS:

(1) clock pattern and clock hands
(1) brad
Pencils and marking pens

LET'S BEGIN:

1. Read *At This Very Minute*.
2. Fill in the numbers on the clock pattern.
3. Cut out the hands of the clock and attach them with the brad.
4. Look at a school clock to see the exact time and set the clock you just made to read the time "at this very minute." Example: If it is 10:30 a.m. when you start the activity, set the clock you made to read 10:30.
5. Think of events in the world that might be happening "at this very minute." Write these things on the lines provided on the clock pattern.
   For example: My mother is at work.
   My sister is at high school.
   My grandfather is reading the newspaper.
   Someone is on an airplane going to England.

NOTES:

Use this book in a unit on telling time.

Related books:
  Someday, by Charlotte Zolotow
  Right Now, by David Kherdian and Nonny Hogrogian
  Do You Know What I'll Do?, by Charlotte Zolotow
  Clocks and More Clocks, by Pat Hutchins

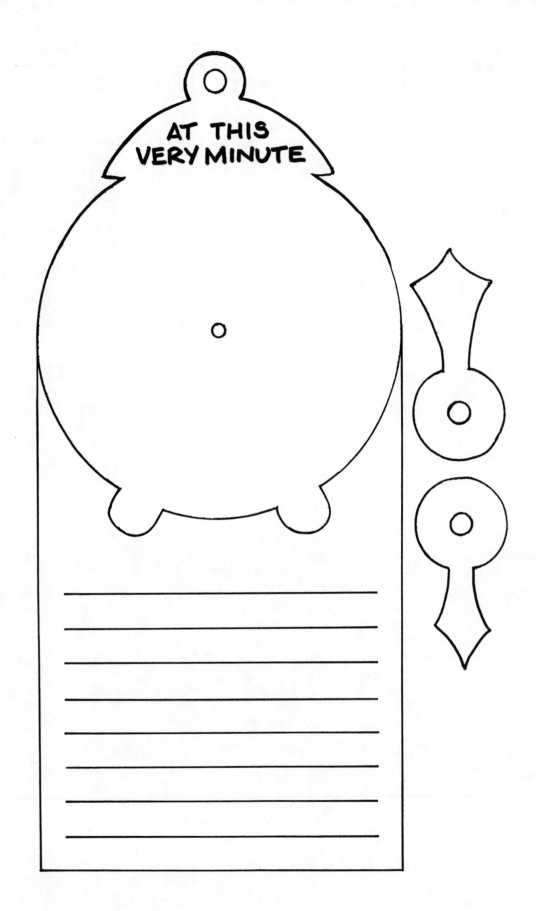

AT THIS
VERY MINUTE

On Market Street

ARNOLD LOBEL

(Greenwillow, 1981)

This imaginative alphabet book contains a collage of wonderful findings beautifully illustrated by Anita Lobel. The book is based on a 17th-century street of shops.

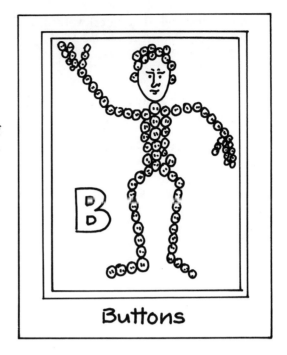

Buttons

PURPOSE:

In this art project children create a collage imitating the artwork found in the book.

MATERIALS:

(1) pattern
Collage materials (e.g., buttons, magazine pictures, pasta, wrapping paper, feathers)
Light blue crayon or marking pen

LET'S BEGIN:

1. Read *On Market Street*.
2. Choose a letter from the alphabet.
3. Write the letter and choose one thing beginning with that letter to decorate the stick figure pattern.
4. Cut out pictures or place objects on the stick figure.
5. Glue the pieces in place.
6. Color the border a pastel blue to match the border in the book.

NOTES:

The following books were written by Arnold Lobel:
Frog and Toad Are Friends
Fables
Mouse Soup
Ming Lo Moves the Mountain

Anita Lobel wrote and illustrated the following books:
A Birthday for the Princess
The Pancake
The Seamstress of Salzburg

Arnold Lobel and Anita Lobel worked on these books together:
How the Rooster Saved the Day
The Rose in My Garden
A Treeful of Pigs

This project can easily be adapted for holiday items (Valentine cards, Christmas decorations, Halloween costumes, Easter eggs, etc.).

This project makes a great cooperative activity. Children apply the materials to a large figure for a bulletin board.

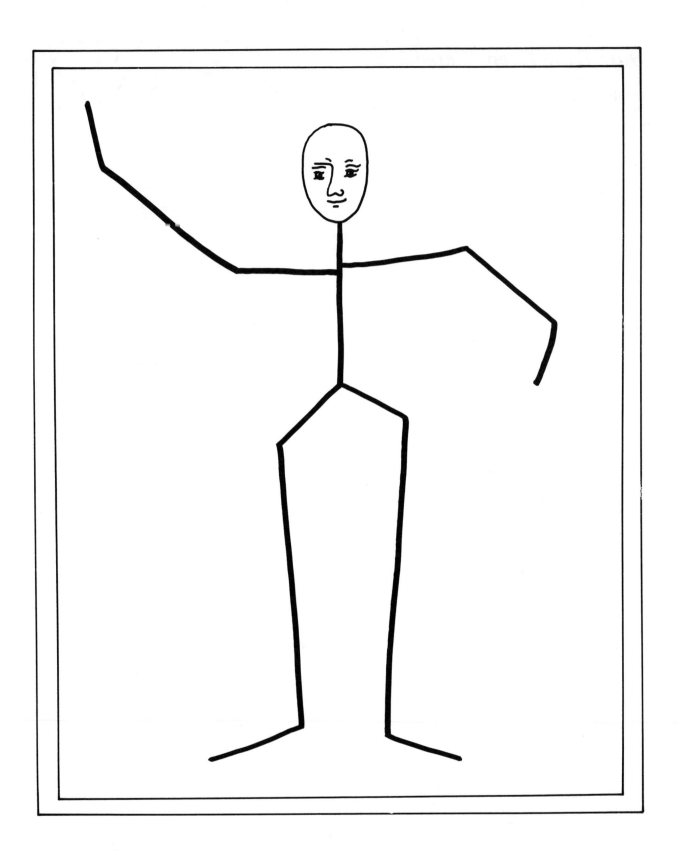

Burt Dow Deep-Water Man

ROBERT McCLOSKEY

(Viking, 1963)

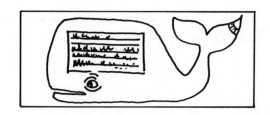

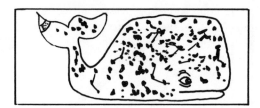

Burt Dow lives on the Maine coast and sets out to sea in his small boat. Out on the open sea, he catches his cod hook in the tail of a whale. He unhooks the line and puts a Band-Aid™ on the whale's tail. Later a storm comes and Burt Dow asks the whale if he could swallow the boat and Burt Dow temporarily. After the storm, to encourage the whale to "unswallow" him, Burt Dow spatter paints the inside of the whale to upset his stomach. Later a whole parade of whales arrives to have their tails decorated with Band-Aids.

MATERIALS:

(1) small Band-Aid
(1) 12x18-inch piece of construction paper
Yellow, black, and pink paint for spatter painting
A piece of screen and a toothbrush for spatter painting
Scissors

LET'S BEGIN:

1. Read *Burt Dow Deep-Water Man.*
2. Cut a large whale shape out of construction paper.
3. Write a summary of the Burt Dow story on one side of the whale shape.
4. Place a Band-Aid on the whale's tail.
5. Turn the whale over and spatter paint the opposite side of the whale to look like the inside of the whale's stomach in the story (see pp. 42-43 in Burt Dow).
6. Display a parade of whales on the bulletin board.

NOTES:

For the whale shape, use colored construction paper in the same colors as the whales on page 57 of *Burt Dow Deep-Water Man.*

Hang the whales in a parade on the bulletin board or wall. You might like to add Burt Dow, the *Tidely-Idley*, and the giggling gull. Review the meaning of the sentence on p. 60 of Burt Dow. "I never did see," said Burt, "so many tons of contentment come from out of such a little old band-aid box!"

Read other books by Robert McCloskey:
Lentil
Make Way for Ducklings
Blueberries for Sal
One Morning in Maine
Time of Wonder

I Want a Dog

DAYAL KAUR KHALSA

(Crown, 1987)

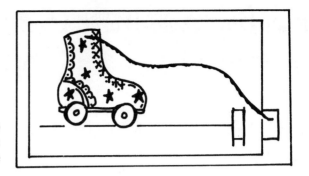

In this humorous story May wants a dog. She comes up with an ingenious plan to get one. Her plan involves taking responsibility for her roller skate in much the same way she would a pet.

PURPOSE:

In this project children make a manipulative to re-enact the humorous theme of the book.

MATERIALS:

(1) 6x9-inch sheet of tagboard
(1) 1x9-inch strip of tagboard
(1) 1x3-inch strip of tagboard
(1) 6x9-inch piece of white construction paper
Scissors
Yarn
Glue
Crayons or marking pens
Stapler

LET'S BEGIN:

1. Read *I Want a Dog*.
2. Trace the skate pattern on the white construction paper and cut it out.
3. Decorate the skate and add details.
4. Cut two 1½-inch parallel slits in the lower right-hand corner of the 6x9-inch piece of tagboard, one inch from the right border.

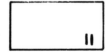

5. Cut a line across the paper two inches from the bottom, one inch from the left border, and one inch from the slits.

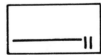

6. Glue the small strip onto the long strip at one end to form an L.

7. Insert the strip of tag through the slits in the lower corner so that there is a tab near the right side. Insert the L tab through the long slit.

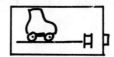

8. Center the skate and glue it on to the L tab. Staple a 12-inch piece of yarn to the top of the skate and glue the other end on the tab.

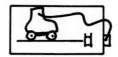

9. Move the roller skate by pulling the skate along the path.

NOTES:

Dayal Kaur Khalsa wrote the Baabee Books, which include:
Bon Voyage Baabee
Happy Birthday Baabee
Merry Christmas Baabee

She also wrote *The Tales of a Gambling Grandma*.

The Doorbell Rang

PAT HUTCHINS

(Greenwillow, 1986)

Ma makes chocolate chip cookies and tells the children to share them among themselves. Each time the doorbell rings, there are more people who have come to share the delicious chocolate chip cookies.

PURPOSE:

    Children act out the story and the mathematical problems of dividing the plate of chocolate chip cookies.

MATERIALS:

    (1) pattern for chocolate chip cookie
Scissors
Black and brown marking pens or crayons to draw chocolate chips
(12) self-stick notes or name tags with the characters' names from the book written on the tags

LET'S BEGIN:

1. Draw and cut out a chocolate chip cookie pattern.
2. Children bring their cookies to the story area.
3. Place the self-stick notes or name tags with the characters' names on individual children. (See notes.)
4. Collect the cookies the children have made.
5. Put twelve of the paper cookies on a plate. The teacher or librarian reading the story will play "Ma" and serve the cookies.
6. Begin reading *The Doorbell Rang*, reminding children to listen carefully for the names on the name tags. "Ma" serves the cookies on the plate. When reading the first page emphasize the names "Victoria" and "Sam" and motion to the children wearing these name tags to come forward and share the cookies with each other.
7. Stop reading and allow time for "Victoria" and "Sam" to manipulate the cookies and divide them equally.
8. Continue reading the story and emphasize the next two names, "Tom" and "Hannah."
9. Stop reading and allow time for the cookies to be divided by four. Continue the story until the twelve characters in the story are represented by twelve students with name tags dividing the twelve chocolate chip cookies.

NOTES:

The names to be written on the self-stick notes or name tags are: Victoria, Sam, Tom, Hannah, Peter, Peter's little brother, Joy, Simon, Cousin 1, Cousin 2, Cousin 3, and Cousin 4.

Act out the story using real chocolate chip cookies. You will need twelve cookies for each reading of the story.

A free film on chocolate, "The Great American Chocolate Story," by Hershey Foods, may be borrowed from Modern Talking Picture Service, 6735 San Fernando Road, Glendale, CA 91201.

A bibliography of books about chocolate can be found in the August 1987 issue of *School Library Journal*, p. 26.

Related books about counting:
    Anno's Counting Book, by Mitsumasa Anno
    Bears on Wheels, by Stanley Berenstain and Janice Berenstain
    Thirteen, by Remy Charlip
    Ten Black Dots, by Donald Crews
    Six Foolish Fishermen, by Benjamin Elkin
    Count and See, by Tana Hoban
    Bunches and Bunches of Bunnies, by Louise Mathews
    How Much Is a Million?, by David M. Schwartz

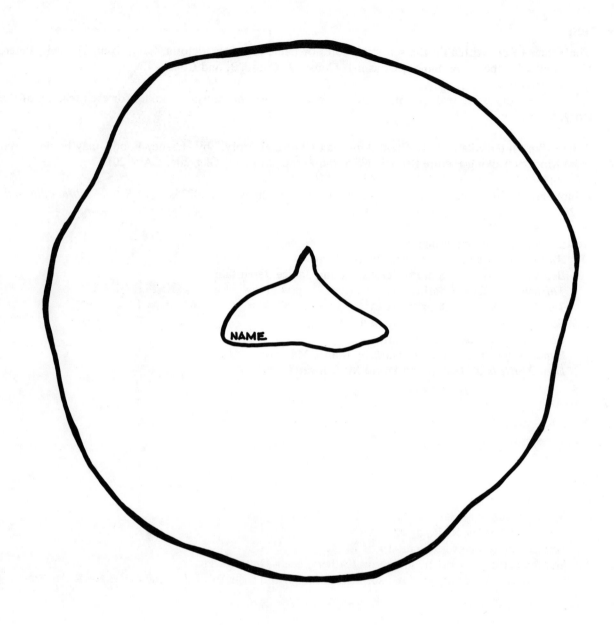

NAME

A Three Hat Day

LAURA GERINGER

(Harper Trophy, 1987)

R. R. Pottle the Third loves hats. He searches for the perfect mate who will share his admiration for hats. This delightful tale ends happily ever after, and R. R. Pottle the Fourth is a lover of shoes.

A Three Hat Day
by Laura Geringer

PURPOSE:

This activity allows children to create an imaginative hat for R. R. Pottle or more for an ultimate three-hat day.

MATERIALS:

(1) R. R. Pottle pattern
Crayons or marking pens

LET'S BEGIN:

1. Read *A Three Hat Day*.
2. Discuss the imaginative hats R. R. might enjoy wearing.
3. Think of a hat for R. R. to wear.
4. Add the hat design to the pattern of R. R.
5. Add details to your hat by gluing on feathers, beads, buttons, etc.
6. Think of a unique name for the special hat design and write this below the picture of R. R. Pottle.

NOTES:

R. R. strolls under a ginkgo tree. Ginkgo trees are ancient trees with distinct characteristics. Studying more about their differences would make an interesting research project for budding botanists.

Discuss the different types of hats mentioned in the book (e.g., fez, fedora, etc.).

Laura Geringer also wrote *Molly's New Washing Machine*.

Related books about hats:
Anno's Hat Tricks, by Akihiro Nozaki
Jennie's Hat, by Ezra Jack Keats
The 500 Hats of Bartholomew Cubbins, by Dr. Seuss
Martin's Hat, by Joan Blos
Caps for Sale, by Esphyr Slobodkina
The Wishing Hat, by Annegert Fuchshuber
The Quangle Wangle's Hat, by Edward Lear

<u>A Three Hat Day</u>

by Laura Geringer

Miss Rumphius

BARBARA COONEY

(Puffin, 1982)

The story tells of the Lupine Lady, or Alice, as she grows from a child to an elderly lady. She reminds her nieces and nephews that in addition to visiting faraway places and coming home to live by the sea, there is a third thing they must do, that is, "Do something to make the world more beautiful."

PURPOSE:

Children hear the story and remember the three things Alice wanted to do. Each child creates a seed packet of lupine flowers and places inside the packet an idea for making the world more beautiful.

MATERIALS:

(1) copy of lupine seed packet pattern
Crayons or marking pens
Scissors
Glue

LET'S BEGIN:

1. Read *Miss Rumphius*.
2. Talk about the lupine flower and show a picture of it. Talk about Miss Rumphius and the lupine seeds she planted.
3. Remember and review the three things that Alice as a child set out to do: visit faraway places; come home to live by the sea; do something to make the world more beautiful.
4. Color the seed packet pattern, cut it out, and glue it to make a seed package envelope.
5. On the slip of paper on the pattern page, write an idea for making the world more beautiful.
6. Cut out the slip of paper and place it inside the seed packet envelope.
7. Individual ideas can be shared.

NOTES:

Plant some lupine seeds and watch them grow. Follow the directions on the seed package.

Locate Maine on a map of the United States since Maine is the location of this story.

This is a good story and project with which to celebrate Grandparents Day.

Related books:
> *A Tree Is Nice*, by Janice Udry
> *Cherries and Cherry Pits*, by Vera Williams
> *I Know a Lady*, by Charlotte Zolotow

I would make the world
more beautiful by

_____

_____

_____

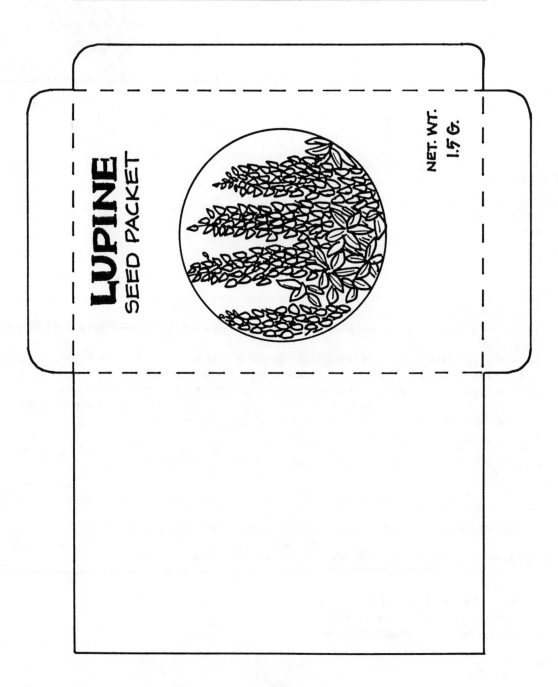

LUPINE
SEED PACKET

NET. WT.
1.5 G.

Frosted Glass

DENYS CAZET

(Bradbury, 1987)

This book is for every child who daydreams in school and for the imagination in all of us.

PURPOSE:

In this activity children imitate the art style in the book and appreciate each person's efforts.

MATERIALS:

(1) 9x12-inch piece of white construction paper
Crayons
Still-life materials

LET'S BEGIN:

1. Read *Frosted Glass*.
2. Pass out construction paper. Assemble a simple flower arrangement similar to the one in *Frosted Glass*.
3. Discuss still life as an art form.
4. Place a * in the corner of one sheet of construction paper. This denotes the piece that belongs to Gregory.
5. Draw a picture with the crayons of the still life.
6. Share the results with the group and hang individual pictures on the bulletin board as the teacher did in *Frosted Glass*.

NOTES:

All the papers could have a * to let everyone draw what they see in the still life.

Other books by Denys Cazet include:
Big Shoe, Little Shoe
Christmas Moon
Lucky Me
Mudbaths for Everyone
Saturday

This book lends itself to a discussion of clouded windows. A good book to help explain why windows fog up is *Rain & Hail* by Franklyn M. Branley.

Related books about self-esteem and art are:
    Mary Ann's First Picture, by Winifred Bromhall
    No Good in Art, by Miriam Cohen

Doctor Change

JOANNA COLE

(Morrow, 1986)

Doctor Change studies spells in his big leather book. He can change himself into almost anything. When a boy named Tom takes a job with the doctor, he finds himself a prisoner in the doctor's house. Tom secretly learns the changing spells, and, by studying the big leather book, he applies these spells to gain his freedom.

PURPOSE:

Each child makes a paper filmstrip showing how Tom changes to escape from Doctor Change. The filmstrip will help children recall the four things Tom changed into.

MATERIALS:

(1) pattern for filmstrip
Pencils and marking pens
Scissors

LET'S BEGIN:

1. Read *Doctor Change.*
2. On the filmstrip pattern page, cut along the dotted lines to make slits on Tom's face.
3. On the numbered strip provided, draw the four things that Tom changed into to escape.
   Draw the cat in box number 1.
   Draw the mouse in box number 2.
   Draw an ant in box number 3.
   Draw a puddle of water in box number 4. Show how the puddle of water dripped out the door.
4. Cut out the numbered strip of paper.
5. Insert the numbered strip through the slits on Tom's face, and slide it from top to bottom to show what Tom changed into.

NOTES:

Related reading:
   Wanda Gág's *Sorcerer's Apprentice*

Teacher resource on folktales:
   World Folktales: A Scribner Resource Collection, by Atelia Clarkson and Gilbert B. Cross

Winnie the Witch

KORKY PAUL AND
VALERIE THOMAS

(Kane Miller, 1987)

Winnie the witch lives in a black house and everything inside is black—the carpets, the bed, the chairs, and the bath. Winnie cannot see her black cat, Wilbur. One day she comes up with a brilliant idea.

PURPOSE:

This activity involves listening and following directions. Children listen and draw as Winnie waves her magic wand and turns Wilbur into a cat with a red head, a yellow body, a pink tail, blue whiskers, and four purple legs—but his eyes are still green.

MATERIALS:

(1) 12x18-inch drawing paper
Marking pens or crayons (red, yellow, pink, blue, purple, and green)

LET'S BEGIN:

1. Read *Winnie the Witch* and stop reading on the page where Winnie "picked up her magic wand, waved it five times and...."
2. Give each child a piece of drawing paper and marking pens.
3. Turn to the next page. ABRACADABRA is the next word you read. (Do not show the children the picture of Wilbur the cat.)
4. Stop reading while each child draws the cat described on this page: "Wilbur had a red head, a yellow body, a pink tail, blue whiskers, and four purple legs. But his eyes were still green."
5. Continue reading to the end of the book.
6. Display all the pictures of Wilbur.

NOTES:

See a similar listening activity in *Creative Encounters*, p. 62, "*The Whingdingdilly*, by Bill Peet."

Related books:
   The Adventures of the Three Colors, by Annette Tison and Talus Taylor
   Dragon Franz, by Elizabeth Shub
   The Great Blueness and Other Predicaments, by Arnold Lobel
   The Mixed-up Chameleon, by Eric Carle

Bibliography

Ahlberg, Janet, and Allan Ahlberg. *The Jolly Postman or Other People's Letters*. Little, Brown, 1986.

Allard, Harry. *Miss Nelson Is Missing!* Houghton Mifflin, 1971.

Balian, Lorna. *Humbug Potion, an A B Cipher*. Abingdon, 1984.

Bang, Molly. *The Paper Crane*. Greenwillow, 1985.

Bayer, Jane. *A, My Name Is Alice*. Dial, 1987.

Blos, Joan W. *Old Henry*. Morrow, 1987.

Bowers, Kathleen Rice. *At This Very Minute*. Little, Brown, 1983.

Brown, Marc. *Arthur's Eyes*, Little, Brown, 1979.

Campbell, Wayne. *What a Catastrophe!* Bradbury, 1986.

Carle, Eric. *The Very Busy Spider*. Philomel, 1984.

Cazet, Denys. *Frosted Glass*. Bradbury, 1987.

Cole, Joanna. *Doctor Change*. Morrow, n.d.

_____. *Golly Gump Swallowed a Fly*. Crown, 1987.

_____. *Large as Life: Nighttime Animals*. Knopf, 1985.

_____. *The Magic School Bus at the Waterworks*. Scholastic Book Services, 1986.

Cooney, Barbara. *Miss Rumphius*. Puffin, 1982.

Crowe, Robert L. *Clyde Monster*. Dutton, 1976.

de Paola, Tomie. *Marianna May and Nursey*. Holiday House, 1983.

Fox, Mem. *Hattie and the Fox*. Bradbury, 1987.

Geringer, Laura. *A Three Hat Day*. Harper Trophy, 1987.

Gibbons, Gail. *Check It Out! The Book about Libraries*. Harcourt Brace Jovanovich, 1985.

Goffstein, M. B. *Our Snowman*. Harper & Row, 1986.

Grifalconi, Ann. *Darkness and the Butterfly*. Little, Brown, 1987.

Hoguet, Susan Ramsay. *I Unpacked My Grandmother's Trunk*. Dutton, 1983.

Hooper, Meredith. *Seven Eggs*. Harper & Row, 1985.

Hutchins, Pat. *The Doorbell Rang*. Greenwillow, 1986.

Jensen, Helen Zane. *When Panda Came to Our House*. Dial, 1985.

Johnston, Tony. *The Quilt Story*. Putnam, 1985.

Khalsa, Dayal Kaur. *I Want a Dog*. Crown, 1987.

Lionni, Leo. *Let's Make Rabbits*. Pantheon, 1982.

Lobel, Arnold. *On Market Street*. Greenwillow, 1981.

Lyon, George Ella. *Father Time and the Day Boxes*. Bradbury, 1985.

Marzollo, Jean, compiler. *The Rebus Treasury*. Dial, 1986.

McCloskey, Robert. *Burt Dow Deep-Water Man*. Viking, 1963.

McPhail, David. *Pig Pig and the Magic Photo Album*. Dutton, 1986.

Mendoza, George. *Need a House? Call Ms. Mouse!* Grosset & Dunlap, 1981.

Morimoto, Junko. *The Inch Boy*. Viking Kestrel, 1984.

Most, Bernard. *Boo!* Prentice-Hall, 1980.

Novak, Matt. *Claude and Sun*. Bradbury, 1987.

Numeroff, Laura Joffe. *If You Give a Mouse a Cookie*. Harper & Row, 1985.

O'Neill, Catharine. *Mrs. Dunphy's Dog*. Viking Kestrel, 1987.

Paul, Korky, and Valerie Thomas. *Winnie the Witch*. Kane Miller, 1987.

Pène du Bois, William. *Lion*. Viking, 1983.

Riddell, Chris. *Bird's New Shoes*. Holt, 1987.

Silverstein, Shel. *Who Wants a Cheap Rhinoceros?* Macmillan, 1983.

Small, David. *Paper John*. Farrar, Straus & Giroux, 1987.

_____. *Imogene's Antlers*. Crown, 1985.

Tejima. *Owl Lake*. Philomel, 1982.

Tokuda, Wendy, and Richard Hall. *Humphrey the Lost Whale: A True Story*, Heian International, Inc., 1986.

Tresselt, Alvin. *The Mitten*. Scholastic Book Services, 1985.

Williams, Linda. *The Little Old Lady Who Was Not Afraid of Anything*. Crowell, 1986.

Index